Brigham Young At Home

Portrait of Brigham Young

Brigham Young At Home

By Clarissa Young Spencer
with Mabel Harmer

Illustrated with Photographs

DESERET BOOK COMPANY
Salt Lake City, Utah

First printing in hardbound edition 1940.
First printing in paperbound edition 1986.

ISBN 0-87579-058-5

Printed in the United States of America   72082

10   9   8   7   6   5   4   3

Brigham Young At Home

LIST OF ILLUSTRATIONS

DEDICATION

To my beloved husband and children
I dedicate this book.
May it inspire you to emulate the life
of my dear father, BRIGHAM YOUNG.

Brigham Young At Home

PREFACE

Brigham Young at Home will be a valuable addition to the history of the home life of pioneer days. Reared in the famous Beehive House, Mrs. Spencer has carried with her through life the patient, loving influence of her parents. As she goes back in memory to the old home, she revives the scenes and varied events which filled her childhood days. She tells of the amusements of the children and the tender solicitation that President Young always had for the members of his family. Simple and straightforward, he was generous and patient, and the day was always begun with a solemn prayer to God. Nature gave to President Young a resolute will, a keen intellect, and a forceful individuality, with which he met the problems of Church and State. In the home, he was happy when he could lay aside the business of his high office, and take part in the play and mirth of the children.

As Mrs. Spencer tells the story of his life, she presents a faithful picture of the family circle, and conveys a fine impression of the part which all took in the daily converse of the old "parlor." The chapters of her book are lovely essays written under the spell of joyful and happy yesterdays. In her golden memories of childhood, she recalls the love and tenderness of her mother, whose manners were singularly simple and graceful. It is all a delightful story, when life was simple and the family hearth was the center of play and happiness.

LEVI EDGAR YOUNG,
Professor of Western History,
University of Utah

Brigham Young At Home

CONTENTS

Brigham Young At Home

LIFE WITH FATHER

The Brighton resort is a lovely little valley perched high in the mountains some 4000 feet above Salt Lake City. The road for the greater part of its thirty miles winds up between sheer mountain precipices, and it was a difficult matter indeed to traverse that rocky way with the cumbersome wagons and oxen or mule teams of the sixties. It was no jaunt for a day's pleasure, this trip to Brighton. When the people went they bundled beds, babies, and provisions into their wagons for a stay of several days. Nevertheless, it was a favorite place for the Mormons to meet in celebration of the Utah state holiday, the anniversary of the day when a band of pioneers had first entered the barren valley and gazed upon it with mixed feelings of hope and consternation as my father, Brigham Young, uttered the momentous words, "This is the place."

On the day of my birth, July 23, 1860, a company of the Saints had made the customary trip to Brighton, and they had no sooner reached their destination than word was brought to Father that my mother had taken ill. To the great disappointment of his people, who felt that no gathering of any sort was complete without their leader, he turned around and went immediately back to the city in order to be with Mother during her ordeal. As I was his fifty-first child, the birth of a baby was far from being a novelty in the family, but his consideration for each of his wives, or any other member of his family, was such that he would willingly forego any pleasure of his own if he could be of any comfort or assistance to them.

Throughout my childhood and early girlhood I had the opportunity of being closely associated with my father. This was somewhat unusual, because in a family as large as ours, consisting as it did of nineteen wives and fifty-six children, it was not possible for each member to spend a great deal of time with him. It was my happy lot to do so because Father had his sleeping room and always ate his breakfast in the Beehive House, which was the home of my mother and her family exclusively.

Let me give you some idea of my father. No child ever loved, revered, and cherished a father more than I did mine, but how could I do otherwise, knowing him as I did? My mother looked upon him as the embodiment of all that was good and noble. He had the affection and tenderness of a woman for his family and friends. He was good to look at, and I fail to recall an instance when he was not immaculate in person and dress. He had well-shaped hands and feet, a clear white skin, and blue eyes—the kind that radiate love and tenderness—and a mouth that was firm, commanding the respect of all with whom he came in contact. Few could resist the wonderful personality that made him so beloved of his people. He was of medium height, rather large, with beautiful light brown curly hair, a high brow that was broad and intelligent, a long straight nose, and a chin that denoted character and firmness.

Each day of my childhood stands forth in my memory as one long round of happiness. The family used to eat an early breakfast, but I always waited until ten o'clock when Father had his, so that I might be served with him. In those days he wore quite a long beard, and it was my duty to tie a bib over it in order to protect it from stray crumbs.

I suppose one of the principal reasons why I enjoyed having my breakfast with Father was because he always had the things I liked. To be sure, there was corn-meal mush and milk, which was no great treat, but there were also hot doughnuts and syrup, codfish gravy which Mother was very adept at making and which Father loved, squabs from the pigeon house, and some little delicacy from our own garden. Brother Staines the gardener was a genius at making things grow under glass, and the first and finest strawberries or other fruits of the season naturally found their way to Father's table. His only hot drink was composition tea made from herbs and spices.

We seldom enjoyed our breakfast in peace, for there was invariably a stream of people calling to see Father about something or other, since he was not only their spiritual leader but their adviser in many temporal problems as well. I rather liked having them come in, however, for they certainly brought a variety of stories and problems. Perhaps there had been an encounter with the Indians with a sad loss of property or even lives. In his efforts at extensive colonization Father had sent settlers to remote parts of the state, and in some instances the savages had become so troublesome that the whites were forced to abandon their new homes. I must confess that I was more excited than grieved when I heard that the redskins were on another rampage.

During the summer months there were frequent reports of the progress of immigrant trains, and if they were in a weakened condition, as was not unusual after their long journey, fresh teams and supplies would be sent out to meet them. Missionaries were constantly being sent out "in the world" to preach the gospel, and this necessitated the arranging of many details, financial and otherwise. The poor of the city would come with their problems, and statesmen would call to pay their respects, but whether it was a poor woman with her tale of sorrow or an important man of affairs, Father received them all with the same consideration and respect and gave them all the help within his power.

After breakfast he would sometimes delight me by saying, "Daughter, go tell Brother Squires to come and barber me," and I would run quickly across the street to the little barber shop on the corner where the Federal Bank Building now stands.

Brother Squires would return with me, bringing his bottles of bay rum and sweet-smelling hair oil, the curling irons, and the big calico cloth to cover over Father. We would all go to his private room for the "barbering," and after Brother Squires had singed the hair (Father never allowed it to be cut as he said it made the ends bleed) he would give me a nice little sprinkle of cologne or bay rum as he finished his work. After a time he left the shop near our home and moved over on Main Street, and when I went over there to have my own curls trimmed I would take in payment a small pail of buttermilk, of which he was very fond.

After he had finished with the barber, Father would usually go to his offices to work until dinnertime, and here, of course, I did not care to go, but sometimes an immigrant train would be arriving, and then I was always eager to accompany him to the tithing office grounds where the wagons would come to rest. When he went out he wore a rather high hat, a Prince Albert coat, and either a green cape or a grey shawl over his shoulders. In the summertime he wore light cream prunella cloth suits—sack coats and trousers, with white shirt and neck cloth and a panama hat. I realize now the wonderful laundry work that went into those suits. They looked like a piece of satin. I remember them so distinctly perhaps, because when they were discarded Mother would make of them little white jackets and skirts trimmed with white braid for my "best" wear.

The tithing office (where in early days the Saints used to bring one tenth of all their produce for the Church) was in the same block as our home, and where the Hotel Utah now stands. The entire block was surrounded by a high cobble-rock wall, and to a big yard within this enclosure came the weary, travel-stained men, women, and children upon their arrival in the city. The covered wagons that had been dragged for long months over plains, high mountain passes, and through deep rivers, bulged at the sides with most of the earthly possessions of the owners, while underneath were strung buckets, kettles, and other odds and ends.

Many of these people had come from the "old country" and could not speak a word of English, but how their faces shone with unutterable joy and thanksgiving of having at last reached "Zion"! Father never left the grounds until every family was comfortably located, for the night at least. The Bishop of each ward was assigned a quota of immigrants, and it was his business to see that they were given a start of some kind in beginning their new home in the West. The settlers who had come previously were always most generous in opening up their homes to the newcomers, having a vivid memory, probably, of the time when they were sorely in need of such hospitality themselves.

Mother always used to say that everyone who didn't have any other place to go was sent to her. Certain it is that to our house came all girls who had arrived in Utah alone. Often they stayed to work for her, and as many of them had come from foreign countries I picked up a generous smattering of Danish, Swedish, German, and Welsh. It seemed that the girls learned the English language more quickly from us children than from any other source, and they reciprocated by teaching us theirs.

Some of these girls knew absolutely nothing about housework, having worked largely in factories before their emigration. I recall one girl who didn't even know how to sew on a button and, by way of contrast, another who knew nothing of any kind of work except the making of buttons, having been practically reared in a button factory. By the time Mother was through training them they were all good housekeepers, but about that time they would either get married or go to work for someone else. Many of these girls were married from our house.

On Saturday afternoons we would often go out to the warm sulphur springs for our baths. These springs were located about a mile west of our home, and Father liked to bathe there because of the medicinal value of the water. I suppose they brought him relief from the rheumatism from which he sometimes suffered. Father, Mother, my young brother, and I would go in the carriage known as the "victorine." It was really only a

light, covered wagon but it had deep springs and
was very comfortable. My parents and brother
sat in the rear seat while I sat up in front in great
dignity with Black Isaac.

Black Isaac, who was Father's first coachman,
was a negro who had been one of the servants of
the Prophet Joseph Smith. After the assassination of the Prophet he had joined Father's household and had come out to Utah in 1847 with the
very first company of pioneers. I believe his wife
came in a later company.

Although there was a great deal of prestige attached to the honor of riding with the only colored
coachman in the city, and while Isaac had been
places and seen things the likes of which no one else
could or would tell me about, still I should really
have preferred being with the other children in the
wagon which was drawn by Jimmy Campbell and
the blind mules. Jimmy was a demure little fellow who worked in our barns and who spent his
spare time sitting out in the shade knitting socks
for his numerous family. There was not much
supervision, and consequently there was likely to
be rather a hilarious time in the wagon, and I
longed to take part in it.

The bathhouse was built with a large pool in
the front part of the building and a number of
small private pools in the rear. These latter were
really no more than large, square-shaped tubs,
being about six feet long and four feet wide. They
were built of wood which had become very dark

from the mineral in the water, and they were elevated a few feet from the floor so that one could stand on a step made of small wooden cleats and conveniently let the water drip off.

Father never went in with the public but used one of the small baths in the rear and also had his own private entrance. I had no scruples about mixing with the others; in fact, the more people I have had around me the happier I have always been, but Mother invariably made me accompany her to another of the small pools. Here again my pleasure in the trip was diminished, for Mother thought that the primary purpose of a bath was to get clean. While I was being duly scrubbed I listened with deep yearnings to the splashings and delighted screams of the children in the front pool.

We would arrive home from the baths just in time to prepare for dinner which was served at 4:30 in the Lion House and a trifle later at the Beehive House.

The Lion House, in which lived the greater number of my father's families, was built in 1856. It was so named from the carved stone lion which rests above the main entrance. The architect was Truman O. Angell who was also architect for the great Mormon Temple, but Father designed the Lion House and supervised the details of the building very carefully. He had learned the trade of carpentry as a young man, and the results of his knowledge are evidenced in such fine features of the home as the easy stair treads and graceful

banisters—quite perfect for sliding upon, except
that such an undignified procedure was never allowed in the presence of Mother or the "aunts,"
and it was extremely difficult to find the great
central hall entirely free from grown-ups.

Another feature of the building that we children enjoyed, whenever we could without interference from the wives, was the dumb-waiter that
was used to carry food, coal, kindling, and other
supplies from one floor to another. We used to
have grand rides up and down, one at a time for
the larger ones and two at a time if we were very
small, but woe to the youngster who was caught on
the waiter when someone wanted to send a load of
kindling up to her apartment. She didn't wait
long enough to find out whether it was her child,
or not, before she administered a healthy spanking.

There were usually about twelve families living
in the Lion House. When the families grew too
large to live there comfortably they were moved
to individual homes, although I recall that Aunt
Emmeline lived there at one time with her brood
of nine, which can scarcely be called a small family.
One wife lived in Provo, one at Forest Farm, and
another at St. George in southern Utah, where
Father usually spent his winters because of the
mildness of the climate.

There were three floors in the house, with a
long hallway running straight through the center
of each. On the upper floor were twenty bedrooms,
where the childless wives and the older boys and

(Photo Courtesy Utah Historical Society)

Lion and Beehive Houses

girls slept. Each bedroom had its own picturesque dormer window, many of them had fireplaces, some had stoves, and all were cozy and comfortable.

The middle floor held the apartments of the wives with small children and the parlor or "prayer room" as it was quite generally known. The floors were the Early American which have recently become popular again, and the woodwork was of native pine painted so skillfully that it is still beautiful today. At the front entrance was a glass vestibule which kept out the cold drafts of winter.

The basement floor was perhaps the most interesting of all. On the west side was the large dining room, where some fifty members of the family sat down to every meal. Can you imagine all of those children watching eagerly to see who would get the first piece of pie? Beyond the dining room were the butteries, kitchen, and laundry.

The laundry was a far cry from the modern affair of today where the housewife has nothing much more to do than turn on a switch. At one end of the room was a brick fireplace where the water was heated in huge brass caldrons. Two large barrels stood along the wall. In one was stored the water for the washing which was softened with wood ashes in lieu of lye or other commercial softeners. The other was used for washing blankets and quilts, and the work was done with a wooden pounder, or "dolly," as we called it in that day. There were high shelves for such aids to superior laundering as homemade indigo blue-ing and homemade potato starch. Each wife had her separate washday so that there was washing going on every day of the week except Sunday. If one of the wives was ill, however, another was always more than willing to come to her aid or put the additional washing in with her own.

There were always plenty of men around to lift the clothes, bring in the water from the pump in the back yard, and assist in every way possible. Father was most considerate of his womenfolk and would not allow them to do any work that could be done just as easily by hired help. The large baskets, which held the piles of snowy clothes, had mostly been made by the Indians and traded to us for food. There was an excellent drainage system for the disposal of waste water, for Father was very particular about sanitation. He never would allow the men to milk the cows until they had washed their hands. I suppose that is one of the reasons why there was so little sickness among us.

The wives also used to take their turns at ironing, but this was done at night by two or three of them so that they could go through the house occasionally and keep a lookout for fire at the same time. During the following day when these women slept, their children would be cared for by some of the other wives.

One wife had entire charge of the kitchen with as many girls as she needed to help her. After the

Golightly Bakery was opened on Main Street we used to buy all our bread there in order to save the members of the family from that particular work. My own mother, who was an excellent cook, presided over the Lion House kitchen from the time it was built in 1856 to 1860, a few months after my own birth, when she moved to the Beehive House and was succeeded by Aunt Twiss.

On the east side of the basement hall were the stone-flagged cellars where ice, butter, milk, eggs, meat, and vegetables were kept. There was a ventilating system which connected the cellars so that the air was always fresh and sweet smelling. Next was the weaving room with its great spinning wheel and weaving loom for the making of blankets and carpets. Neither the wheel nor the loom was ever idle for any great length of time, and very fine articles they turned out too. I cut up some of our home-woven blankets and used them for my own babies for many years. They were much softer than any I could purchase at the stores.

At the north end was the schoolroom where Aunt Harriet Cook taught the children of the family for many years. Later it was turned into a recreation room and was the scene of merry entertainments during the long winter evenings. Father had a small platform erected for our dramatics, and many a fairy princess and valiant knight, dressed in costumes pieced together from four and twenty bedroom closets, tripped back and forth to the admiration of brothers, sisters, and mothers. There were large steel hooks upon the wall for the pulling of molasses or vinegar candy and a small stove for the popping of corn. There were never any dull moments in our family, I assure you. What one child couldn't think of, several others could, and Father never left anything undone that could add to our happiness.

The outside of the Lion House was finished in cream plaster, which with the white woodwork and green shutters made a very lovely combination. It was beautiful to me then, as now, and I never stand within its rooms that I do not hear once more the echo of happy childish voices and gaily tripping feet.

It seems strange to many that this co-operative idea of living could have been so successful among our families, but Father believed that it would have been feasible, even, to extend the plan to include the entire community. In one of his sermons in the Tabernacle he said that he would like to see houses built for a group of one thousand people and having one central eating place. Then instead of a woman having to get up and "fuss around a cookstove she would have nothing to do but go to her work." The dining hall he had in mind would seat five hundred people, and his idea of serving them was a rather quaint version of the modern roteria. He suggested that if a person at one end of the hall wanted a beefsteak he could telegraph his wants to the kitchen and the order would be conveyed back by means of a small railroad. When everyone was through eating, the dishes were to be slipped under the table and run back to the ones who washed them. Knowing that dishwashing was a job that all the women in the community would avoid, he suggested that " a few Chinamen could do that." He concluded by saying that "half the labor necessary to make people moderately comfortable now, would make them independently rich under such a system."

I must not leave the Lion House without a word about our splendid gymnasium. Along the full length of the west side of the house ran a huge porch, and here Father had placed every contrivance available in that day. We had horizontal ladders and straight ladders, horizontal bars, back boards to straighten our shoulders and make us walk upright, jumping ropes, wands, hoops, roller skates, wooden swords, dumbbells, swings, and big balls to kick and roll about. We had regular teachers to instruct us in gymnastics, fencing, and solo dancing. It was probably because of our training in dancing that the girls of our family were in such demand for "fairy" or ballet dancers when the Salt Lake Theatre was opened. Needless to say, we adored our gymnasium, and besides all the fun we had we gained poise and developed fine, strong bodies. The roof of the porch was used for sleeping quarters by the older boys and girls in the summertime when the upstairs rooms with their single dormer windows were likely to become rather warm.

Holding almost as high a place in our affections was the family swimming pool, or "fount," as we called it. It was located just back of our schoolhouse and was about twenty feet square and four or five feet deep. A clear stream of water from the near-by canyon supplied the water which ran in and out again by means of small troughs. The water was warmed only by the summer sun, but it was always quite comfortable. At least, I never remember of anyone's staying away from the pool on account of the water being cold, as long as his mother would allow him to go in. Our bathing costumes were made with an eye to modesty rather than beauty and consisted of linsey dresses and pantalettes for the girls and shirts and overalls for the boys. Incidentally, the "fount" was used also for baptismal services.

Our bathhouse was made out of an old discarded band wagon which had benches along the sides. Father had a roof put over the top, pegs put along the sides for our clothes, and drainage holes bored in the bottom. With these few alterations it made an admirable dressing room.

I have been asked several times if there were not an underground passage near the Lion House which was used by Father and others to hide in during the raids against those who were practicing polygamy. I feel reasonably sure that the rumor came from the fact that at one time a large canal

ran under a portion of Father's property. I know
that when my sister Mira built her home just
north of the Beehive House it was necessary to
have brick arches constructed in the foundation
for the canal water to flow through. The old canal
has been abandoned for many years, but the arches
still remain. I have heard recently of someone's
discovering this canal and concluding that it was
a secret passage, but in following its path a complete barricade of earth and bricks was encountered which was impassable. So falls to earth another absurd and sensational chapter about these
historic homes and my beloved father. But to return to the house and its people. About seven
o'clock in the evening Father would go to his room,
light a candle in the tall, brass candlestick, come
into our sitting room across the hall, and say
quietly, "Time for prayers." No matter what we
were doing or who was there, we dropped everything and followed him through the long narrow
hall and into the parlor of the Lion House. Uncle
Joseph Young and Uncle Lorenzo Young, who
lived near us, frequently came in to join in our
family prayers and would often be sitting in their
places in the parlor when we arrived.

Father would step to the glass cupboard, take
down the prayer bell, go to the door, and give three
distinct rings. After a moment he would put the
prayer bell back and take his place by his brothers
in the center of the room. In a very short time
the patter of feet would be heard in the long hall-

way upstairs and down, and the children would come tripping in to be followed by their mothers with a more sedate tread. Father and his brothers sat on the west center part of the room. On their right, in an honored place, sat Aunt Eliza R. Snow, and on around the room were the rest of the family, each wife having her own place with her children about her.

Father usually discussed the topics of the day, and then we would all join in singing some familiar songs, either old-time ballads or songs of religious nature. Finally we would all kneel down while Father offered the evening prayers. One distinct phrase in his prayer I shall never forget it so impressed my childish mind was—"Bless the church and Thy people, the sick and the afflicted and comfort the hearts that mourn."

One night after we had all been seated Father took out his pocketbook and drew from it a sheaf of crisp, new ten-cent bills. He called all the children about him and handed a bill to each one. It looked like a hundred dollars to me, for we saw very little actual money, all of our needs being supplied for us. From that time on I never missed evening prayers if it were at all possible for me to attend.

After the prayers the members of the family would disperse to their apartments, where the younger children would be put to bed and the wives perhaps visit with one another in their various sitting rooms. During the winter evenings we would pop corn or make molasses candy, always saving a plate of the latter for Father if he were absent, as he was very fond of it. Ernest and Art, my brothers, would get a pan of snow over which the candy could be cooled very quickly. Then it was great fun to snap it between one's teeth. Father liked to eat the fresh popped corn in a bowl of rich milk, and he also loved sugar candy, which he would often ask my sister Fanny to make.

After Arbogast opened his candy store on First South Street, Father would have Mother put a white earthen bowl in the center of a napkin and tie the four corners over the top. Then he would send me off with it over my arm like a basket to Brother Arbogast with the words, "Tell him I want fifty cents worth of stick jaw but I want him to wash his hands before he breaks it." When I returned, Father would take a portion, put it in the oven to soften, and then we would all "fall to." My, how good it was! Real "store" candy.

Whenever anyone went out for the evening, he took his own lamp and placed it on a table near the glass vestibule. Upon his return he carried the lamp back to his own room, and the one who returned to find but one lamp burning on the table locked the door for the night.

On Sunday evenings the older girls were permitted to entertain their beaux in the parlor. The oldest members of the group became rather famous as the "Big Ten," because there were just that number who seem to have grown up about the

same time. There was only the one large parlor
for them to entertain their young men in, and
twenty did seem rather a large number when
there were only four corners, so, one evening, the
happy suggestion was made that some semblance
of privacy might be obtained by turning down the
coal-oil lamp that stood on the table in the center
of the room. A second thought was that the light
might be more effectively dimmed by placing a
barricade of books around it. The main idea, anyway, was to get rid of the light, so everyone lent a
hand, and soon there was but one shaft of light
that played upon the ceiling where no one minded
it. The couples then went back to their chairs and
the sofa, which seemed so much more cozy in the
semidarkness.

All went very well for a time until the door
slowly opened, and there stood Father with a
candle in his hand. He gave one look around the
room and then walked to the table where he removed the books one by one until the proper light
shone forth on faces that would have preferred
the darkness for a different reason now. Then
turning to the very much subdued group, he said,
"The girls will go upstairs to their rooms, and I
will say good night to the young men."

He could be stern when occasion demanded but
he was the wisest, kindest, and most loving of
fathers. His constant thoughtfulness for our happiness and well-being endeared him to all of us.
The bond between my father and me was as close

as if I had been his only child, and I am sure that each of the other children felt the same way. I shall always be grateful that I was born his daughter.

THE BEEHIVE HOUSE

The only home I ever knew, until six years after my marriage, was the Beehive House. No matter where I go or where I live, this will always be my real home, for it holds the memories of my father, mother, brothers, and sisters, and is enshrined in my heart as a place where love and perfect harmony existed.

The home was undoubtedly planned in Father's mind through happy memories of the beautiful colonial buildings in Vermont, his birthplace. Being a natural architect, he was largely responsible for the plans of the house, assisted by Truman O. Angell, an architect of great ability. It was somewhat smaller than the Lion House, and the two of them were joined together by a hallway and by Father's offices.

To me, the Beehive was the more beautiful of the two houses. It was a large square house with white pillars reaching to the second story in true colonial fashion. The thick adobe brick walls were plastered and then kalsomined in a pale yellow. The large windows were adorned with lovely green shutters, and the big front door was of solid oak with a silver doorknob.

Considering that it was built in the midst of a wilderness and now stands in the center of a mod-

(Photo Courtesy Utah Historical Society)   Eagle Gate and Rock Wall at the Brigham Young Estate

ern city, it has not been greatly changed. The green shutters have gone, I am sorry to say, and the rear part of the house has been raised to a full two stories, but other than that, it appears, from the outside, much as it did when it was built in 1854. The original front door now stands on the east side and with it the quaint doorbell that used to peal forth at night, when all the house was still and dark, with a most startling effect.

The house was first occupied by Mary Ann Angell Young, who lived there until 1860 when she moved to the White House, and Mother, with her seven children, moved over from the Lion House. She boarded all the men who worked upon the estate, usually about eighteen in number, as well as the girls who assisted in our home. Father never allowed us to call anyone who worked upon the place "servants." They were always "the men or girls who helped with the work." The Beehive House was also used for entertaining distinguished visitors who came to our city, or any other guests to whom Father wished to show hospitality.

Because it was built largely for entertaining, the rooms were spacious and beautifully furnished. There were two parlors, one upstairs and one down, both on the southeast part of the house. The lower room, which also served as our sitting room, was charmingly decorated with the walls in a soft green shade, lace Nottingham curtains at the windows, and an ingrain carpet on the floor. It was here that Father always ate his breakfast.

The upper room was the more elegant of the two and was called the "Long Hall," and with a length of fifty feet, it was truly "long." It had a fine coved ceiling ending with beautiful plaster moldings. The furnishings included two Lady Franklin stoves, chairs, two large couches, which could be put together to make a bed—and frequently were at conference time—white lace curtains with rose lambrequins on gold cornices, and a pale grey carpet decorated with bunches of roses and green leaves. Not the least of its attractions were the large looking glass in its gold frame with the basket of flowers underneath fashioned from colored shells, and the two chandeliers fitted with their coal oil lamps.

Through the length of the house on the main floor ran a wide hall which was painted in blocks about fifteen inches square to represent Tennessee marble. On the other side of this hall, just opposite to the sitting room, was Father's bedroom. It was a fine, light, airy room, exactly sixteen feet square. For the greater part the furnishings were simple but well-built pieces made by William Bell, our cabinetmaker, a washstand, secretary, and a few comfortable chairs. At the head of the bed was a small table with a carafe covered with glass and his high brass candlestick with a box of matches.

A wall cupboard on the west side was always a point of interest to me because, from its recesses, I could usually depend upon Father to produce

(Photo Courtesy L.D.S. Church Information Service)   The Long Hall — Beehive House

(Photo Courtesy L.D.S. Church Information Service)   Brigham Young's Bedroom in the Beehive House

rock candy, a few raisins, or some other delicacy for the pocket of my apron. The walls were painted in a subdued pink, and during cold weather a fire always burned in the Lady Franklin stove. A door on the west side opened into his private offices.

From the front hall a long staircase led to the upper floor, with a landing at the end of the first flight. On the wall by this landing hung a large picture measuring about eight by ten feet and made of dark yellow parchment framed in oak. It was divided into squares, and in each square was a pen drawing representing some part of the story of the Bible. It had hung there for as long as I can remember, and when we moved from the Beehive House, the "Bible Picture" was left behind as it was too large to take into any house of ordinary proportions.

There were two stairs from the landing, one of which led to the second floor and the other to an inside room used for closet purposes. The only light in this room came from a tall, narrow window with fascinating tiny panes of glass which opened out looking down directly into the front hall. Whenever I went into this room, I loved to imagine that I was a fairy princess imprisoned in a tower and waiting breathlessly for my rescuers. In time I would hear some knight's step below me, but usually it would be my brother Feramorz calling that Mother wanted me for something or other.

Another door on this same landing led to a lovely bedroom called the "Blue Room," and the third door led to the southwest room, which was mine. It was directly above Father's room and had the same proportions, sixteen feet square. The walls were painted pink, and the woodwork painted to simulate bird's-eye maple and done so well that the paint still remains after more than eighty years. On the south wall was a large window reaching to the floor, which we used as a doorway to the big porch that runs the length of the front of the house. In summer we had our beds here, sheltered from the east sun by canvas curtains. In later years, when I grew up to young womanhood, and the boys would come at midnight to serenade me, this porch was a most convenient place to step out onto, listen to the songs, and thank the serenaders. I would gather my "wrapper" close around me and stand in the shadows of the veranda while the romantic ballads of the seventies floated up on the night air.

A humorous incident of the porch and serenaders comes to my mind. We had a young girl staying with us by the name of Lottie Claridge, who was teaching in Father's schoolhouse across the street. When I heard the boys singing, one night, I went to the back hall and called to her to come out. After they had gone, I took her back to the hall and asked her if she could find her way to her own room. She said, "Yes," and so I left her and climbed back into bed. I was just dozing when I heard a voice faintly calling my name, "Clint, I'm lost. I'm against something warm and afraid I will fall."

I went back to the hall and asked her what was the matter, and with tears in her voice she begged me to come and help her. I lighted a candle and went back to her. Shall I ever forget it! She had walked forward until her foot struck something, then she had stepped up, found herself against a very warm wall and was afraid to step off for fear she might fall. The step was her steamer trunk in front of the big kitchen chimney, which was warm and had terrified her. When I had rescued her, we both sat down on the trunk convulsed with laughter, but Lottie never went adventuring through the halls in the dark again.

From the second floor the stairway became a spiral leading to the attic, two small rooms with large half-diamond-shaped windows on the east and west ends. One of these I used for a "studio," after I became interested in painting. Under the sloping roof of this third floor hung great bunches of Black Prince grapes, which Mother would put there in the fall of the year to dry and use for raisins.

Atop the house is the square pedestal on which stands the large beehive which gave the house its name. It was undoubtedly suggested by the state's first being known as the territory of Deseret, meaning industry, of which the beehive is a worthy symbol.

Behind the sitting room on the first floor were

two small rooms, a buttery and a bedroom, then a large dining room known as "the men's dining room," because the workmen on the place were served there, and beyond that the big kitchen with its tin-lined sink, tall cupboards reaching from floor to ceiling, and the great range, almost constantly in use.

At the north end of the house was the family "store" kept by John Haslam. The store had a private door that opened into the back hall of the Beehive House, but to my knowledge it was never used by anyone but Father. The rest of us used the outside door on the east. In this store were kept staples, notions, drugs, dried peas and apples, calicoes and candy. Naturally, what stands out in my memory is the candy kept in large, square jars. I used to go into the store with a small piece of cotton cloth and ask John to please put a few drops of cinnamon oil on it. Then I would take out raveling by raveling and chew it. It was like eating cinnamon candy, a flavor which I love to this day. Whenever I would go into the store alone, John would give me a lump of white sugar. He was very good to me, and I shall never forget him.

Each wife had her charge account here, as well as one at the Zion's Cooperative Mercantile Institution, the leading dry goods store of the city, where fancier items could be purchased than those carried in the little family store at home. As far as I know the wives were not limited in either account, although I suppose they knew enough to

Family Store in the Beehive House

(Photo Courtesy L.D.S. Church Information Service)   Kitchen of the Beehive House

keep their purchases within reasonable bounds.

Whenever I wanted a list of things from the town store I would go to Father rather than to Mother for permission to get them. It was a trifle easier to obtain his consent, and he didn't bother to scrutinize my list quite so carefully as Mother did. One day I brought for his approval a long list of things that began with "corn plasters." Father glanced at it and then smiling at me quizzically said, "Well, daughter, if corn plasters is at the top, I guess the rest of it must be all right, so just go ahead." Thereafter I put everything I could think of on my list before I brought it to him.

Downstairs was only the cellar. But such a cellar! Will I ever forget those cupboards filled with huge stone jars of preserves, the swinging milk shelves with the ten-quart pans and the thick cream that I loved to see Mother skim with a skimmer and not a spoon, the stone floor that was so pleasantly cool in the summer and the big, highly polished stone slab on the long table where Mother made huge batches of piecrust. There was a wonderful smell to that cellar that can never be approached in the modern cement basement.

In spite of all the help that Mother had, it seemed that there was always some corner of that house that demanded her attention. Usually my own days were quite carefree except when housecleaning time came around, and no one was too young or too small to escape that cataclysm. All the rooms in both houses were covered with carpets, some "store" products, but the greater number of them home woven, and every spring all of those carpets had to come up and be cleaned. Mother used to take hers up in the fall as well because they had so much wear. Oh, for one good vacuum cleaner in that day! After the carpets had been cleaned, fresh straw was laid upon the floors, and the carpets tacked down again. This was where the work for us younger children came in. We would go to the tannery, get small pieces of leather and cut them into tiny squares. Then when the men tacked down the carpets, we handed them a piece of leather to put under each tack so that the carpet would not come over the head of the tack.

There was no season for the sewing of carpet rags. The womenfolk were eternally at it. It was their fancywork, and many an afternoon or evening the wives would gather in one sitting room and the older daughters in another while their nimble fingers cut the rags, sewed them, and wound them into large balls. Later the balls would be taken down to the weaving rooms in the Lion House and made into the really beautiful carpets that covered most of our floors.

Altogether, the Beehive House held fourteen rooms, but in spite of this, what with emigrants and visitors, we were always crowded to capacity. During "conference" time, when great numbers of the church membership gathered in Salt Lake for this semiannual event, we were practically crowded out. Every house in the city had an over-

flow of relatives and friends, in the early days, and
we were certainly no exception to the rule.

I especially remember Brother Fishburn's choir
members who used to come down from Brigham
City, twenty-five strong, to sing at the meetings
and to sleep in our beds. In order to make room
for them, Mother would put us children out on
the "deck" to sleep. The deck was the attic above
the hall that connected the two houses and was
used only for storing books containing church
records. The women of the choir invariably
brought along a number of new babies but, as
they always took them off to church with them, I
didn't mind that so much as having to give up
my bed.

They couldn't have known my real feelings toward them, for they were always most cordial to
me. On one occasion Brother Fishburn invited me
to go up and sit in the choir seats. Mother demurred, saying, "I don't believe she had better go
today—she isn't dressed up very much." No such
delicacy of feeling bothered me, however, for, looking the crowd over coolly, I replied, "Oh, I don't
know. I think I look about as well as the rest of
these people do."

All the laundry work for the Beehive House
was done in a little one-room building just west
of the outer cellar door. I can not remember
when Sister Barker did not wash and iron for us.
She was a dear little old lady and used to tell me
stories of her former home in England, all so dif-

ferent from this new country. I was usually on hand bright and early to watch her begin her day's work. The fire was always ready when she arrived, and the big copper boiler would be full of boiling water which had been softened with wood ashes.

Sister Barker's hands used to fascinate me, as she worked, they were so big and strong and the water made them so crinkly. She would take basket after basket of snowy, white clothes and hang on the line and then, after all the better clothes were washed, would gather up the blankets and quilts, put them into a big barrel, and pound them with the old dolly until they were clean. She would change the water frequently by pulling a plug out of the barrel to let the water out, and how I loved to see that stream pour like a foamy waterfall into the square hole in the floor into which all the waste water was run.

The little house was also used for other purposes. When the boys would go out shooting rabbits, they would bring them back to the laundry to clean and skin them before handing them over to Mother to be cooked. She never used any part except the hind legs, and I couldn't bring myself to eat even that, but the boys considered rabbit a great delicacy.

My brother, Feramorz, together with Richard W. Young and Heber J. Grant, frequently used the laundry room for making ice cream. Each boy furnished part of the "makings" and Mother showed them how to cook the custard, in which art they became quite expert. After it had cooled they would put it into a pail with a tight lid, set this within a larger pail, and cover with salt and ice. Then they would take turns twisting and turning the inner pail until the cream was frozen.

Of course I never had any part in this procedure, but would sit on the back steps patiently watching and waiting until the lid was raised and a spoonful taken out for "sampling." I would usually get a chance to lick the spoon, and that was about all. I was not very popular with the boys, nor were they with me. I do not think I should have liked them any better, at that time, had I foreseen in Heber a future president of the church, in Richard W. a brigadier general, and Feramorz an honor student at Annapolis.

Near the laundry house was the old pump that supplied all the water for the two houses. That pump handle was going from morning until night, and I daresay there was cause for that groan that issued each time the handle was raised.

Disposal of waste was quite a problem for so large an establishment, but it was handled with every regard to the best in sanitation that was possible in that day. Near the kitchen door was a large box six feet square, sunk about nine inches in the ground, with an outlet in the bottom that emptied into the cesspool. It was several years before we had running water in the house and pipes for waste water, but at that we had them

long before they were in common use. At the rear
of the two houses was an ash pit built with a rock
wall about four feet high. This was emptied once
a week after a good wetting down. Great quantities of lime were used for any refuse that could
not be carried away from the place. In order to
keep the house free from mice, Father had a small
square opening left in the foundation on the east
side so that cats might come and go at their will.
He would never permit a dog or cat in the house,
but kept a fine dog, Queenie, up at the barn.

Back of the Beehive House were the many buildings where the work went on that supplied our
daily needs, and each has its pleasant memories
for me. The old carpenter shop at the corner of
canyon road was filled with wonderful shavings
—full of life and sunlight, it seemed to me. Mother
would send me with a sack to gather some for
lighting the fires, but before putting them in I
would go through them very carefully and pick
out the long ones to use for ringlets. I was sure
they really looked like golden curls hanging down
my back, and I would trudge home with my sack,
quite proud of my find.

Nearly every morning I would go to the pigeon
house for two pigeons for Father's breakfast.
Brother Hamilton Park, our overseer, would go
up into the loft, bring them down, and wring their
necks. I always turned my back and shut my eyes
while this was going on, then I would take them
by the legs, very gingerly, and carry them home

to Mother who would make them into a dainty dish.

A rod or two north was the shoeshop where old Brother Reiser sat all day long making or repairing our shoes. I wore these homely shoes all during my childhood, but didn't mind as I knew nothing better. Brother Reiser was a gruff old person with a Welsh accent, but I rather liked visiting him because I could always depend on his giving me a piece of shoemaker's wax to chew. I was very careful never to let Mother or Father see me chewing the wax, for I knew quite well that they would disapprove very vigorously. I can't imagine now how I ever liked the dreadful stuff but I know that in those days I much preferred it to the spruce gum the boys would bring home from the canyons.

Beyond were the blacksmith shop, the flour mill, the barns, corrals, the gardens, and the schoolhouse. To the north was what we called the "upper garden," a fine orchard of apple, peach, black walnut, and pear trees. The garden and the schoolhouse were in such proximity, and the ripe autumn fruits so tempting, that a high board fence had to be built in order to keep the children outside and the fruit inside. Even this was not sufficient to keep out the big boys, so an added protection was provided in the shape of a big, bald, live eagle, who seemed to realize fully that it was his duty to patrol the garden. The eagle, I must say, proved quite effective.

I seldom visited this garden without my father unless I was holding on to Brother Staines's hand for old "Baldy" certainly made me nervous as he looked at me coldly with his eagle eye. The beehives were also located in this garden, and bees have never been any respecters of persons. However, the gardener was always most kind to me, and if I didn't dare venture inside he would bring a choice bit of fruit to me at the gate.

The other workmen around the place were equally kind, and especially do I remember the rides I enjoyed here and there on the shoulders of old Daddy Sewell who milked the cows. He was a great fellow over six feet tall and had a queer mop of light, curly hair—almost corkscrew curls, they were so long. He used to go from the barn to the Lion House with a large pail of milk in each hand and with me astride his shoulders. We must have made a great procession with old Queenie, the dog, bringing up the rear. Anyway, they were the grandest rides I ever had.

Of the entire place, the spot dearest to my heart was the corner where the old discarded stage-coaches were kept. Here, the sisters who were near my own age and I played with our dolls and had "theatres" during the long summer afternoons. There was always a bit of discarded finery in some closet or other that we might acquire for costumes, if we begged hard enough, and the dolls made a patient if unresponsive audience.

Life for us was one continual joy. There were

so many of us to plan picnics in the hills, picking wild flowers, hunting pretty mossy places to play with our dolls, and build houses with sticks and stones, that the days never seemed long enough to do all the things we planned. Our play dishes were mostly gathered from broken dishes discarded from the kitchen, or sometimes a bit of looking glass, and what was lacking we supplied with little molded bowls made of good clean mud and baked in the sun. I had a great passion for pretty rocks and pebbles and used to fill my pocket with them, much to Mother's annoyance, as the weight often pulled and tore my skirt from my waist.

Mother's great pride was the garden that enhanced the Beehive House and lent its fragrance to the air throughout the long summer days. It was fenced off with lattice work standing about three feet high, and we children certainly respected that bit of choice ground. One beautiful cherry tree heavily laden with snow-white blossoms stands out in my mind. How I longed to pick some of those blossoms to put into a vase, but such action was strictly forbidden until the blooms became full-grown ox-heart cherries. Memories of the privations of pioneer life were still too vivid to permit of such wastefulness. Some of the lilac bushes my mother planted still stand by the east wall. Near the small gate was the loveliest locust tree I have ever seen, which my grandmother Harriet Page Decker Young had planted in the ground, where she first camped, from seed brought from

Nauvoo. All summer long its gracious branches shaded our kitchen door. I was heartbroken when this tree, with its sacred memories, was cut down.

In the big "upper" garden fruit and vegetables grew in abundance. We had several gardeners to take care of this garden, but when the time came for picking the fruit, which must be cared for quickly after it had ripened, the families were called on the job.

During strawberry time the different families were notified of their days for picking and the portion of the patch assigned. When our turn came Mother would put every child and maid available to work, because she needed so many for her large establishment. She would have ten-quart pails, baskets, and cups ready the night before, and by 4:30 in the morning we would be wending our way to the garden, two good blocks from our house.

We would pick into the cups and when they were full, empty into the larger baskets. I would go on ahead and pick the biggest ones, never suspecting that I didn't do a full share of the work. This part was fun, but walking home later in the hot sun decidedly was not, and after breakfast there would be those pails and pails of berries to be picked over. After eating them in the patch for three hours, I would lose my taste for them, and the hulling would be real work. I remember saying to Mother one day, "I hope I never see another strawberry as long as I live!" I am thankful that kind Providence did not take me literally at my word. Mother would cook gallons of them into jams and preserves, and, of course, we had all we could use fresh on the table with lovely thick cream.

Mother's shortcakes were without an equal, and we all just loved them—Father especially. As long as the berries lasted, we would have our days for picking and we also had appointed days for working in the peas, raspberries, and cherries.

When the peaches were ripe everyone was sent to the bowery—a large open-air affair with a roof made of branches—to dry peaches. The men would bring them in from the orchard in bushel baskets for us girls to cut, stone, and lay out on clean tables to dry in the sun. Some of the folks would leave the peelings on, but Mother was very particular and would never allow us that privilege. She was also very careful to have her peaches covered with mosquito netting. It used to look as if there were acres and acres when they were all spread on the tables in the sun.

Sometimes we would add a little variety to the monotony of peach drying by making "peach leather." This strictly original product was made by mashing the peaches to a smooth pulp, adding some sugar, and spreading the mixture out in thin layers on a clean cloth. When dried it would be cut into pieces and made a very delicious "chewy" concoction.

In one part of the garden was a big cellar where vegetables were stored. One day Father's man-

ager sent two of his boys up there to sprout potatoes. After a time the attention of one of the
boys wandered from the potatoes to a number of
kegs that were stored in the rear of the cellar. "I'll
bet there's cider in those kegs," he remarked to
the other. The brother agreed that the kegs probably held cider but couldn't see what difference it
made to them.

"I'll show you," said the more ingenious one
and, going out, he returned with a number of full-
grown onion tops. The next step was to find a keg
with a plug in the top that could be withdrawn, and
when this had been accomplished both boys lay on
top of the barrels and drank cider through the
onion reeds until they actually rolled off. For once
in their lives they had all the cider they wanted
and more than they could manage with comfort.

There was something wonderful to me about
the upper garden. Its beauty, the nearness to the
mountains, the sparkling streams of water, the
getting together of the different families—the
older ones telling their experiences and we children planning for our play hours. I do not seem
to remember any great hilarity and believe now
the reason was the indescribable influence of Father's private burying ground, which lay on the
east hill just beyond the garden. Several of our
family were buried there and we could see the
head boards or stones from where we sat under
the bowery tending to our fruit. Sometimes Father
would drive up through the garden to see how

things were coming along and to try out the flavor of those wonderful peaches and pears. His influence was felt constantly. He was so affectionate and understanding that we always looked forward to his coming among us and partaking of our pleasures and fun.

The entire estate was surrounded by a cobblestone wall nine feet high, with gates placed at convenient intervals. Father had a threefold purpose in having this wall constructed. In the first place it was built as a protection against floods. The stream from near-by City Creek Canyon at times swept down the street and was capable of doing some real damage to the garden and of flooding the basements of the houses. The second reason was that employment might be furnished for the emigrants until permanent work was found for them, and finally the wall was useful as a protection against the Indians who were still troublesome during the fifties and sixties.

Each member of the family had his own key to the gates, for they were kept locked after a certain hour in the evening. Just in front of the office was a guardhouse where someone was always on duty to keep out intruders and maintain a sharp lookout for Indians as long as that procedure was necessary.

The main entrance to the estate was the "Eagle Gate," so named from the large wooden eagle which stood guard on its pinnacle. The eagle was designed by Truman Angell and carved by Ralph

Ramsey from five blocks of wood: one for the body, another for the neck, two for the wings, and the fifth for the beehive upon which it was mounted. The whole was held firmly together by pieces of iron. At that time there was no way to get through to City Creek Canyon, except through Father's grounds, and so his permission had to be obtained by the settlers when they wished to drive through the Eagle Gate and on up to the canyon for firewood.

There was a legend in the old days that every time the eagle heard the noon whistle blow, he would leave his perch, fly straight down State Street to the old wooden watering trough, get a drink of water—or something, and fly back again. I sat many a time with my feet in the carriage house stream, waiting for the bird to fly, but apparently I was always called to dinner at the wrong time, for I never had the pleasure of seeing him in action.

When the street under the eagle became city property, the old bird was left in peace, but when the street had to be widened for the use of electric cars, it seemed that he was about to be doomed, since there was not room for the cars to pass under the arch. We were all most anxious to preserve our old friend, and my brother Don Carlos, who was then church architect, drew plans showing how the gate could be enlarged and still remain as a loved landmark.

The eagle had grown somewhat dilapidated under the snows of thirty years, so it was sent east to be rejuvenated with a beautiful copper covering. He was reinstated with appropriate ceremonies in 1891 and was stuffed with numerous papers and relics before resuming his position as guardian of the gate and our loved home.

FATHER'S WIVES

I believe that a finer group of women never lived together than my father's wives. They co-operated with one another to a remarkable degree, and to each one of us children the "aunts" were almost as dear as our own mothers were. I loved them all with good reason, for they all treated me with the greatest affection.

Much has been said and written about the great ingenuity my father displayed in organizing and directing the migration of the Mormon pioneers to the Rocky Mountains—the greatest trek of its kind ever undertaken in this country. I believe that he displayed a resourcefulness almost as great in keeping contented and happy more than twelve wives under one roof. For happy they really were. Undoubtedly at times there were small frictions and jealousies, but they very seldom showed on the surface, and our home was as peaceful and serene as any home could be.

They cared for one another's children, they gathered together to sew rags for the carpet which one of them might be in need of, they shared their joys and sorrows with each other. Where one was weak, another was strong and gladly gave of her strength to the weaker one. Just one instance of helpfulness that might have been a common, everyday occurrence. The families were coming down Big Cottonwood Canyon one day where the way is very steep and where the river rushes along by the edge of the road over huge jagged rocks. In one of the wagons a lively child of a year or so escaped from its mother's arms and fell from the side of the wagon into the rushing stream below. Aunt Martha, who was riding with father two wagons ahead, happened to see the accident, and quick as a flash she leaped from her place down into the stream and saved the child who would otherwise surely have been dashed to a sudden death among the rocks.

The harmony that existed in the Lion House, however, could only have been brought about by very careful planning and directing. All the wives had equal rights and privileges and each was, in turn, expected to do her share in keeping the establishment running smoothly. Each wife took care of her own apartment and her own children and assisted in doing other necessary work around the place.

Those who had no children—of whom there were several—naturally took a heavier part in the running of the entire establishment, such as supervising the cooking or working in the weaving and spinning rooms. Each one worked, also, according to her talents. While Aunt Zina and Aunt Eliza gave much of their time toward building up the church, Aunt Twiss was queen of the kitchen in the Lion House and Aunt Susan Snively managed the home at dear old Forest Farm.

For this reason it is very difficult to attempt to write impartially of Father's wives, for while some of them were energetic in doing public and church work, others were very quiet and retiring, and I cannot hope to do justice to this latter group. All of them had many fine characteristics and sterling qualities.

While I knew all of the nineteen wives who survived at Father's death, space will permit my giving sketches of only a few of them.

Too much honor cannot be paid to Mary Ann Angell—"Mother Young"—who shared with Father all the poverty, trials, and persecutions suffered during the early days of the Church before the Saints came to Utah. The wife of Father's youth had been Miriam Works, who had died at an early age, leaving two little girls. On her marriage to father, Mary Ann Angell took these children to rear and bore a large family of her own besides. They had been married only a short time when Father volunteered to go with the men of "Zion's Camp" to take help and supplies to the suffering Saints in Missouri. He was gone for several months, and during this time she supported herself and the two little girls entirely by her own efforts.

During the early days of persecution in Kirtland, Ohio, she was alone a great deal of the time while Father was forced to flee and remain in

hiding for his very life. Many times she stood by
in fear and anxiety while apostates and anti-Mor-
mons searched the house for her husband. Finally the persecution became so severe that he fled
to Far West, Missouri, where she followed later
as best she could with the five young children—the
two girls of Miriam Works and the three of her
own which had been born to her by now.

They found conditions in Missouri no better
than they had been in Ohio. Their lives were being
continually threatened, and finally they were driv-
en out entirely and forced to make their way
back to the banks of the Mississippi River. This
journey from Far West to the Mississippi was
one of the most heartbreaking ever undertaken
by the members of the Church. It rained and
snowed a great part of the way, and often the
ground was so low and swampy that they walked
through mud up to their ankles. Very seldom did
they have adequate shelter wherein to spend the
night. By the time they reached the river the rain
had turned to snow, and they made their beds for
the first night on the riverbanks with six inches of
snow on the ground and without even the comfort
of a fire, which they found impossible to light.

Throughout this terrible journey, Mary Ann
did not even have the help and protection of her
husband the greater part of the way, for he left
his family eleven times in order to return with
teams and help others who were in a still worse
plight than themselves.

They had no sooner reached the river than Father was called, along with the other apostles of the Church, to go on a foreign mission to preach the gospel. It never occurred to any of them to question this call. When Father left he was so ill that he could not walk, without assistance, the thirty rods to the river to embark on the boat, and Mary Ann was just recovering from the birth of a baby then only ten days old.

Mary Ann Angell came of the strictest Puritan parentage, and naturally the introduction of polygamy was a great trial to her, as it was to my father. He tells of standing by the grave of one of the departed brethren and wishing that the lot of the dead man were his own. The burden of polygamy seemed harder than the hand of death. Nevertheless, they both accepted the principle as coming from a prophet of God, and when Father was married to the other women who became his wives before the journey west, it was with the full consent of Mother Young.

She bore all the trials and hardships of the exodus with true courage and bravery. During the first winter she remained with the Saints in Winter Quarters near where Omaha, Nebraska, now stands. She now had seven children to care for, but, in addition to this burden, her benevolence to the poor was such that it was remembered for years afterwards. During her first year in the Salt Lake Valley she lived in a little hut close to the "log row" where Father's other wives and chil-

dren had their home until better quarters could
be provided. In later years she lived in the White
House, a beautiful and spacious home about a block
east of the Lion House.

Naturally the one who stands out foremost in
my memory is my own dear mother, Lucy Decker
Young. She was truly a wonderful character, as
many others besides myself could testify. She had
been given a rigorous New England training in
her childhood, rising at five o'clock with the other
members of the family in order to have the housework done by seven and be ready for the "real"
work of the day—spinning, weaving, sewing, and
making soap and candles. She said that she never
remembered seeing candlelight at night. When
darkness came, they went to bed. She often remarked that when she had her own family, none
should be forced to arise at any certain time. They
should have their required or natural sleep and,
as I remember, she held to this resolve as far as it
was possible to do so. It was probably because of
her early training that she was such a marvelous
housekeeper and was able to accomplish such an
extraordinary amount of work in later years.

Mother became Father's first plural wife when
she was married to him in June, 1842, four years
before the journey to the West was begun. At the
time the first company came she was ill and unable to travel, but in September of the next year,
1848, she made the journey to Salt Lake. As she
and her baby weighed less than one hundred

pounds they were allowed to ride in the wagon most of the way. Most of the company walked.

That same wagon box was her first home in Utah for many months. In after years it was made into two tables, which are now in my possession. She then moved to the old fort, where nearly all the pioneers lived during the first year in the valley in order to have protection from the Indians. Her next home was in the log row, a row of rooms built in the form of the letter L and made of logs put together with mud plaster. All of Father's families, with the exception of Mother Young, lived there at that time, and one room was used as a schoolroom for the children. Later Mother moved to an adobe house where the Church office building now stands and from there to the Lion and Beehive Houses. Father gave her the title to the Beehive House on the condition that no matter what his reverses or financial conditions might become she would never mortgage or give him the home, and she never did.

I never heard her complain of the long, hard trip across the plains, but rather she expressed thankfulness that she was permitted to come to Utah and deemed worthy to cast her lot with the Saints in the wilderness, as it indeed was at that time.

The picture of Mother as I remember her in my childhood days is a very lovely one to me. She was of medium height with beautiful brown eyes and hair as fine as silk. As I think back, I never remember her with her hair untidy or uncombed. She used to part it in the middle, comb it down over her ears, then braid it in about eight or nine strands and loop it up at the back in a soft "bob," as it was called then. She had two dimples in her cheeks, and her smile to me was adorable. She did not have a beautiful nose, but a nose that seemed to fit in with the rest of her features and that made it seem just right. Without exception, she had the loveliest, whitest skin I have ever seen and pink cheeks that added to her charm.

Besides taking care of her own family of seven, she boarded all the men who worked on the estate, and the number of meals alone that she served in one day would have been enough to stagger a less valiant soul. The hired men had their breakfast at seven and were away to their work before the family breakfast was served at eight, just early enough to allow the children to get ready for school. At ten o'clock Father was served and at noon the men, and the family again ate separately. Two suppers in the evening finished the day's meals unless Father had special guests in later, which he often did. Of course there were always two or three girls helping with the work, but still Mother did a good share of it herself. She thought nothing of making fifty mince pies at one baking or of freezing ten gallons of ice cream.

Sometimes I was amazed at the things Mother was called upon to do in the way of managing the home and preparing big suppers for Father's guests. When I said something of this to her one day she replied, "If your father wasn't the most wonderful man in the world, I couldn't do it." She adored Father, but there wasn't a jealous hair in her head. Some of the other wives undoubtedly were jealous at times, although they had no reason to be, for Father treated them all just as much alike as he possibly could, but Mother never was. She had previously made a most unhappy marriage, and the contrast between that and her later happiness was so great that she appreciated it to the fullest extent.

In spite of the many demands upon her, she always had time to do the little personal things for me that a child loves. She would brush my curls and make adorable little dresses for me of pink or blue delaine. Even my underwear bore fine embroidery that must have taken many hours of her time.

Some of my fondest memories of Mother are in connection with our weekly bath night. The Saturday night bath has come to be something of a joke in this day of built-in bathtubs and running hot water, but even a weekly bath was no small accomplishment in the sixties. The boys would bring the water from the pump in the back yard and fill the big copper boiler which had been placed on the kitchen stove. Then the big washtub was brought in, and as soon as the water was warm it would be transferred from the boiler to the tub and the boiler refilled until all seven of us had taken our turn in the washtub.

After we were all through we would go into the big front room and draw chairs up to the stove. Mother would take me in her arms, draw her blue, checked apron over my feet and legs, and rock me while she told us all stories. How I loved it! It was all very cozy and homey with the soft light from the fire and the lamp playing on the green-tinted walls and Mother's sweet face. She told the same stories and riddles over and over again, always starting with the story of the "Golden Bull," but I enjoyed them just as much at the hundredth telling as I did the first time.

One of my most treasured keepsakes which belonged to Mother is the "Kensington tapestry," which came into her possession through a rather peculiar circumstance. During the days of the gold rush in California in 1849 a great many covered-wagon trains passed through Salt Lake City on their way to the gold coast. These people had sold or left all of their property in the East, believing that riches inevitably awaited them in California once they were successful in reaching that place. Unfortunately, a wagon in one of the trains caught fire, and nearly all of the contents were burned. The one small trunk which was saved contained a beautiful hand-woven piece of tapestry representing Mary and Jesus during the flight into Egypt. It measured five by three and one-half feet.

In despair over the plight of his family, the

owner of the wagon came to Father and offered to sell him the tapestry for fifty dollars worth of food, enough to see them safely through to California. Food was still very scarce in Utah in those days, but Father knew that the family could not possibly go on without provisions so he bought the tapestry. It hung on the walls of the Beehive House throughout all my childhood days and came into my possession upon my mother's death. When it was nearly one hundred years old I had a glass covering put over it in order to give it better protection.

Aunt Clara Decker, Mother's own younger sister, was the wife who accompanied Father in the first company of 143 pioneers who blazed the trail into the Salt Lake Valley for the great number who were to come later. Because of this, she is often called "the pioneer wife." At first it had been thought wisest to take only men upon this arduous journey, since not even their exact destination had fully been decided upon, but as Heber C. Kimball was not very well at the time it was necessary for his wife to go with him. Of course she did not care to be the only woman in the company, so two others came as well, Clara and her mother, Harriet Page Decker Young, who was at that time the wife of Father's brother, Lorenzo Young. My mother and Aunt Clara were, of course, her children by a previous marriage. Clara had been married to Father in 1844 when she was only sixteen years of age, and she was still but a girl in her teens when she first gazed upon her "home" in the Salt Lake Valley, a barren sagebrush waste with scarcely a green thing in sight.

I remember Aunt Clara best for her loving, sympathetic nature. She could have mothered whole multitudes if it had been necessary for her to do so. In addition to her own four children she reared the children of Margaret Alley, one of Father's wives who had died young and left two little ones. She also had under her protection at the Lion House her own younger sister, a woman and her son by the name of Farnham, and a young Indian girl whom they called Sally.

Aunt Zina D. Huntington was the "Doctor" of the family and a very remarkable woman in many other ways. She was one of the four wives of the Prophet Joseph Smith whom Father had married upon his death in order to give them his name and protection in making the journey to Utah. She was a very ardent member of the Church and had received many spiritual manifestations during the time she lived in Kirtland as well as in her later years. She arrived in Salt Lake with some of the very first companies and lived in tents and wagons until log houses could be built. She was the mother of only one child by Father, but she also reared the three children of Clara Chase, one of Father's wives who had died in childbirth.

One of the many practical experiments which Father undertook in the development of the commonwealth was the raising of silkworms, and Aunt

Zina was placed in charge of this work for the Church. She had direct charge of a large cocoonery and mulberry orchard belonging to Father and raised the cocoons very carefully, attending to them with her own hands. A very good grade of silk was manufactured at this time, of which many pieces are still in existence.

She took a very active part in directing the women's organizations of the Church and traveled many times to southern Utah and other distant parts when such travel meant a journey of several days' duration in a rumbling wagon over rough roads. She was an eloquent speaker, and at one time when she delivered an impromptu speech at a mass meeting, a woman reporter wrote of the occasion, "I raised my eyes to her standing just before the table we were using. Suddenly, as though her words struck home like an electric shock, several gentlemen sitting at my right hand, clutching the arms of the chairs, started as though they would rise to their feet, their faces burning with the truths they heard, their eyes fixed upon her fearless and uplifted hands. I can never forget that moment. It was more than eloquence, it was inspiration."

In 1879, Aunt Zina made a trip to the Sandwich Islands where she did a great deal of missionary work and was received most enthusiastically. She was gone for two years and upon her return was met at the station by thirty ladies in carriages who escorted her to the Lion House, where a reception was held in her honor. In 1891 she was made vice-president of the National Council of Women. This was unusual, because it was in a day when honors were seldom accorded to Mormons.

It is as the "Doctor," however, that she is known best. She had very little training but had a great deal of natural ability which was put to use not only for our own family but for many others throughout the city. She officiated at the arrival of hundreds of babies, including all that were born in the Lion House. Many of the poor people of the city depended upon her for advice and comfort as well as for physical ministrations, and she seemed to have a never-failing supply of all three.

The medicines which Aunt Zina kept on her shelf were the common ones of the day—camphor, ipecac, hot drops (and whatever they were, they were exceedingly hot), mustard, and composition tea. In times of contagious diseases we wore around our necks the supposedly potent asafetida bag and hung sulphur sheets over the doorways. Raw onions in plates were sometimes kept around the rooms in order to absorb the poisons that might be in the air.

The composition tea was used by Father not only as a medicine but for his usual hot drink, since our religion teaches us not to use ordinary tea or coffee. I still drink it myself and have given the recipe to hundreds of friends. Here is Father's own recipe for it: 4 oz. each of ground bayberry, poplar bark, and hemlock; 2 oz. each of ground ginger, cloves, and cinnamon; and 1 oz. of cayenne pepper. I take a small bit on the end of a spoon, fill the cup with hot water, and use plenty of cream and sugar.

When Father was suffering with rheumatism, Mother would wrap his knees in red flannel, put the hot drops on them, and give him composition tea. I used to carry a small pail of it cold to the Tabernacle for him to drink in place of water when he was preaching from the stand. Some years ago one of my friends called upon me, and as she was somewhat chilled from the cold weather I made her a drink of the hot composition tea. It seemed to be just what she needed, or at least what she thought she wanted, and she drank so much that she became ill. Since then she has always referred to it as "Mormon Highball."

On the rare occasions when we needed a professional physician, old Dr. Bernhisel was called to the house. He had a peculiar belief that all food should be eaten without salt, and he not only practiced this queer notion himself but insisted that his family follow as well. Think of longing for just one pinch of salt when there were literally square miles of it in the valley! When poor Mrs. Bernhisel became so weary of saltless food that she could stand it no longer, she used to come to our house, and Mother would prepare a plate of good food for her, well seasoned with salt.

Naturally, healing by faith and administration was commonly practiced in our home since it is

one of the principles of the Church. I sometimes
think that Father must have had just a touch of
superstition in his make-up, for at one time when
my brother Fera had stepped on a nail, Father
asked the boys to go out to the barn, find the nail,
and bring it into the house. When they had done
so he handed it to Mother saying, "Grease it well,
Lucy, and keep it in a warm place and the foot will
be all right." And in a short time the wound did
heal. Perhaps by faith. Who knows?

Down at the lovely Forest Farm lived Aunt
Susan Snively, associated in my mind with all the
delicious things to eat that a visit to the farm invariably brought forth. Others of the wives lived
there at various times, but I seem to remember
Aunt Susan best so I suppose she must have been
the superior cook. The farm was about three miles
south of our home, and the road out was such a
beautiful drive that we used to go out by the
wagonload whenever we had the opportunity. Father was very proud of the farm and loved to take
visitors out there, especially those from the East.
I was always very careful to be dressed up and in
the near vicinity on such occasions so that I often
had the opportunity of driving out with them. I especially remember the day I rode out there in the
company of the charming actress, Julia Dean
Hayne.

A long lane with shade trees on either side led
up to the house, which was a homey place with a
gabled roof and a great porch that ran all the way

around. Hollyhocks and roses bordered the porch, and a great profusion of other flowers grew in odd nooks and corners of the lawns. All of our butter, eggs, milk, and cheese came from the farm, and it must have taken a tremendous amount to supply an establishment the size of ours. The blooded stock was kept out there also, really breeders, I suppose, although we children never heard mention made of anything of the sort.

Another wife who was a wonderful housekeeper was Aunt Eliza Burgess. She lived in Provo for some years and kept a house there for Father so that he would have a place of his own in which to stay while he was making Church visits to that part of the state. I spent one entire winter with her in that delightful town, and a very pleasant winter it was too. She sewed many little pieces of dainty clothing for me when I was a child, and when I was grown she endeared herself still further to me by making my wedding cake.

Quite the opposite from these "homemaker" types of women was Aunt Amelia Folsom, whose elegance was partly responsible, I suppose, for the frequently circulated statement that she was Father's "favorite wife," a statement that was entirely without foundation. I loved to go to her room, because she had such beautiful cut-glass bottles of lovely-smelling bay rum and cologne which I might sniff to my heart's content. Her father had given her some very fine jewelry which she would permit me to play with on the floor. I would empty it all out of the box and then put it back in again, piece by piece, admiring each jewel as I did so and longing for the time to come when I would be grown up and perhaps have some of my own.

She was an accomplished musician, being able to play the piano and to sing, so naturally she was very much in demand at home entertainments. As she had no children and therefore had more time on her hands than some of the other wives, she used to put a great amount of beautiful handwork on her underwear. I loved her "modesty skirts"—short petticoats that reached from the waist to the knees—because they were so dainty with their crochet trimmings, and yearned for the time to come when I could wear them myself. In fact, I wore the queer things for years after my marriage simply, I am sure, because the desire had taken such firm root within me.

Aunt Harriet Cook was the schoolteacher of the family. She had received an excellent education in the East before she joined the Church, and when the Lion House was first built she taught the children of the family in one of the basement rooms which was completely fitted up for the purpose. She was also a highly skilled tailoress. I was a frequent visitor to her room as well as to Aunt Amelia's, but instead of giving me jewelry to play with, she would set me to work cutting carpet rags. She knew, I presume, that I would soon tire of this work and leave, which I would.

No one at the house appealed to me more greatly
than Aunt Eliza R. Snow. She held a most honored
place in our household and indeed in the whole
community, for it is doubtful if the Church has
ever produced any woman who was her superior.
She was a plural wife of the Prophet Joseph Smith
and had been crushed with grief at his martyrdom.
Father had married her in Nauvoo but, although
he always provided a home for her, she was his
wife in name only.

Early in life Aunt Eliza showed great promise
as a writer. At the time of the terrible destruction
of Missolonghi by the Turks she wrote a poem
commemorating the event that received a great
deal of favorable notice throughout the literary
circles of the day. Shortly afterward when the
deaths of John Adams and Thomas Jefferson occurred on the fourth day of July, 1826, she was
requested by the press to write their requiem,
which she did, composing the poem of sixty lines
in the short space of five days. Best known of all
her writings, however, is the inspirational Mormon hymn, "Oh, My Father." She continued writing throughout her lifetime and published nine vol-
umes after her arrival in Utah.

She was slight and fragile and always immaculate in dress. I see her now in her full-skirted,
lace-trimmed silk dresses, with her dainty lace
caps and a gold chain around her neck, looking
for all the world like a piece of Dresden china.
She always sat on Father's right at the dinner

table and also in the prayer room. He valued her opinion greatly and gave her many important commissions, especially in relation to the women's organizations of the Church. Her numerous duties in this capacity earned for her the quaint title of "Presidentess."

Among the many duties which this fragile little woman undertook was that of establishing the "Woman's Cooperative Store and Exchange" at my father's suggestion. He remarked in his sometimes outspoken manner, "The women can take hold and do all of the trading for these wards as well as to keep a big loafer to do it. It is always disgusting to me to see a big fellow handing out calicoes and measuring ribbon. I would rather see the ladies do it. Let them do this business and let the men go to raising sheep, wheat, or cattle."

The Relief Society had first been organized in Nauvoo, Illinois, with the Prophet's wife, Emma Smith, as president and Aunt Eliza as secretary. When the work became general throughout the Church in 1866, the latter was made president and held the position for twenty-one years, a responsibility which entailed a great deal of traveling and executive work. One of the first Relief Societies organized was for the purpose of caring for and teaching the Indian women who were often hungry and nearly naked. It was called the Sisters' Indian Relief Society.

There is no doubt but what Aunt Eliza was also the power behind the throne in organizing the

"Retrenchment Society," although Father is usually given the entire credit. She was very extravagant in her own mode of dress, invariably putting yards and yards of material into her skirts and trimming her gowns as elaborately as possible, but she could not bear to see a like extravagance in the younger generation, her feelings on the subject, indeed, amounting almost to fanaticism. I haven't the least doubt but what she was entirely sincere in the matter, evidently believing that what was quite all right for a woman of her judgment and experience would fill the heads of the young girls with vain and idle thoughts.

On one occasion Father had given each of the older girls a beautiful grosgrain ribbon sash some nine or ten inches wide. One of the girls, Phoebe, had laid hers out on the bed with her party dress in anticipation of an evening dance. When she went into her room just after dinner, the sash had disappeared, and naturally Phoebe was filled with indignation. Seeking out her mother on the verge of tears, she told of the disappearance, ending with the statement, "I know that Aunt Eliza has taken it." Her mother attempted to persuade her differently, but Phoebe was so sure that she waylaid Father in the hall on the way to evening prayers and made the same statement to him.

"All right, daughter, we'll see," Father replied mildly, and as Aunt Eliza came by on her way to the prayer room he stopped her and said, "Phoebe has lost a sash. Have you seen anything of it?"

"Yes, President Young," she said.
you wouldn't approve of anything so fr⸗
your girls so I put it away."

"Sister Eliza," said Father, "I gave t⸗
those ribbons, and I am the judge of what i⸗
and wrong for my girls to wear. Phoebe is to
her sash."

So peace and the sash were restored for t⸗
one occasion, but there came a time when Fathe⸗
called all of the girls into the parlor and announce⸗
that they were becoming entirely too adept in following the fashions of "the world" and that he
would like them to modify their manner of dress.
Flounces were to be curtailed, bangs were no longer
to be frizzed, bustles were to be subdued; in fact,
they were to retrench in all the vanities and frivol-
ities of the world and set an example for the rest
of the daughters of Zion to follow. To be sure the
girls had been in the habit of loosening their
tight skirts before they went into the prayer room
so that the bustles appeared less conspicuous, but
this was not enough. The bustles were to be perma-
nently subdued.

A regular organization was effected called the
"Retrenchment Society," and my sisters agreed,
although with no great enthusiasm, to give up the
frills so dear to the hearts of young and pretty
girls.

This was not the first time that Aunt Eliza had
trifled with the whims of Madame Vanity among
the pioneers. During the fifties she had been a

leader in an effort to stabilize women's dress in
the territory, which had resulted in the Deseret
Costume, a hideous affair consisting of bloomers
and full skirts, without trimming, hoops, or trains.
The costume was short lived, but it helped to pave
the way for the society which was later formed.

Before long the group grew to include other
young women of the city outside of our own family
and in time to extend throughout the entire
Church. Today it is a strong organization known
as the Young Women's Mutual Improvement Association, but its aims have changed with the times
and personalities, and now it deals largely with
religious instruction and with directing the rec-
reational activities of the young people of the
Church.

THE UTAH WAR

The famous African explorer, Captain Burton, in his book *The City of the Saints* said in his description of Father: "Such is his Excellency, President Brigham Young, prophet, revelator, translator and seer—the man who is revered as king or kaiser, pope or pontiff never was; who, governing as well as reigning, long stood up to fight with the sword of the Lord, and with his few hundred guerillas, against the then mighty power of the United States, who has outwitted all diplomacy opposed to him; and finally who made a treaty of peace with the President of the great republic as though he wielded the combined power of France, Russia and England."

Captain Burton referred to the "Utah War," when through diplomacy, cunning, and not only one "act of God," but several, an army of the United States was kept out of the territory long enough for misunderstandings to become cleared and a great catastrophe averted.

This dramatic episode in Mormon history began during the July 24 celebration of 1857. Great numbers of the people had traveled through Cottonwood Canyon to the lovely resort at Silver Lake. The pilgrimage had begun early on the morning of the twenty-second, and by midnight of the following day, according to statistics, 2,587 people, 468 carriages and wagons, 1,028 horses and mules, 382 oxen and cows had completed the journey.

Just over the ridge, in nearby Little Cottonwood canyon, the granite was already being taken out for the foundation of the great temple, the erection of which was the pinnacle of all their fondest hopes and dreams. What a comforting thought that the Saints had at last found a place of refuge where a mighty temple could be reared without fear that it would be torn down by mobs and its worshippers driven from their homes as well.

Great preparations had been made at Silver Lake for the occasion. Three boweries had been built with plank floors for dancing. Five bands and numerous choirs were with the merrymakers, and all was in readiness for a fitting celebration in honor of the tenth anniversary of the founding of Deseret.

On the morning of the twenty-fourth, Father requested the Saints, because of their large numbers, to attend to prayers in their tents. The Stars and Stripes had been unfurled at sunrise, and throughout the morning there were programs, singing, dancing, and visiting. Among the attractions was the parading of Captain John W. Young's company of light infantry, fifty boys between the ages of ten and twelve, resplendent in bright, new uniforms and aptly called "The Hope of Israel."

At high noon the gaiety of the scene was rudely

interrupted by the arrival of four travel-worn horsemen, O. A. Smoot, Porter Rockwell, Judson L. Stoddard, and Elias A. Smith. They went into conference with the Church leaders at once, and before evening their tidings were announced to the people. An army of twenty-five hundred from the States was marching toward the Territory, the Government had canceled the mail contracts, and numerous far-fetched rumors concerning the Mormons were being circulated in the East. Smoot and Stoddard had ridden from the States in twenty days in order to bring the message with all possible speed.

After the first shock there was little or no confusion. Father told the people to go on with their merrymaking, and the day's festivities ended with a dance, as had been originally planned. A decade earlier he had stated that "if our enemies will let us alone for ten years we will ask no odds of them," and the ten years had passed. The people he led believed that he had spoken truly.

In Father's mind, however, was immediately shaped a great resolve. He would prevent the army from entering the Territory if it were at all possible. Failing in that, the people should not be driven from their homes—they would leave them voluntarily and set fire to them before they should fall into the hands of the enemy. To the members of his council he said, "We have built cities in the East for our foes to occupy; our very temples have been desecrated and destroyed by

them but with the help of Israel's God we will prevent them enriching themselves with the spoils of
our labors in this mountain retreat."

It was thought that General Harney, the Indian fighter, would, in all probability, be in command of the advancing army, and during the day
Brother Poulter composed the following lines
which the people quickly joined in singing:

> Squaw-killer Harney's on the way
>   Doo-da, doo-da
> The Mormon people for to slay
>   Doo-da, doo-da, day.
> Then let us be on hand
> By Brigham Young to stand
> And if our enemies appear
> We'll sweep them from the land.

The Saints were at a loss for a time to understand why an army of such proportions should be
descending upon them, but gradually a few facts
came to light. Chief among the apparent reasons
was a letter written by William W. Drummond,
formerly a judge in the Territory, charging that
the Supreme Court records had been destroyed
with the direct knowledge and approval of Father,
that a change of governors was imperative, and
that no executive could be installed without military aid. He also hinted that the Church authorities had been responsible for a number of murders
and indicated that lawlessness and rebellion existed generally. Some color was lent to his charges
by the reports of two other men, one a disgruntled

mail carrier who had lost his contract to a Mormon.

It is not reasonable to suppose that the United States Government would have gone to the enormous expense of sending an army on a march of over one thousand miles on such flimsy and unverified reports, if there had not been a deeper reason. In the light of later events, that reason became quite apparent. John B. Floyd, who was Secretary of War at that time, was a rank secessionist, and there was no better way in which he could aid his cause than to send a large part of the Union forces off to this inaccessible region, leaving Governmental arsenals and military stores unprotected in many Southern states. It has also been suggested that there were probably some money-grabbing contractors who used their influence to have the army on the march.

Whatever the causes, the venture was destined to cost the Government somewhere between fifteen and twenty million dollars and to go down in history as "Buchanan's blunder."

The Church leaders lost no time in shaping a course that would keep the soldiers beyond the boundary line of the Territory, at least until communications could be sent to Washington and the misunderstandings cleared. If they failed in this, the plan was to journey south to other wildernesses or mountains, leaving their homes and fields in ashes. On the nineteenth of August thousands of the Saints met in the Tabernacle and pledged their support to Father and his counselors in whatever course they elected to pursue.

A few days previous, Colonel Robert T. Burton was instructed to start toward the east with a company of 160 men. The ostensible purpose was to give aid to emigrants, but in reality they were to keep close watch on the approaching army and report all movements. They went as far as the Sweetwater and at Devil's Gate camped within half a mile of the advance army. Here they cached some of their provisions and sent an express on to the Platte. Men came frequently on mustangs to bring word to Father of all that went on, in spite of all the cold and danger that such a ride involved.

On September 1, Captain Van Vliet arrived in Salt Lake City in an effort to purchase supplies for the troops. He says: "On the evening of my arrival Governor Young, with many of the leading men of the city, called upon me at my quarters. The governor received me most cordially and treated me during my stay of six days with the greatest hospitality and kindness. In this interview he made known to me his views with regard to the approach of the U. S. troops in plain and unmistakable language. The governor informed me that there was an abundance of everything I required for the troops but that none would be sold to us. I told them frankly what I thought would be the result of their present course, that they might prevent the force from entering Utah this year but that next season the U. S. would send sufficient troops to overcome all opposition. The answer to this was invariably the same, 'We are aware that such will be the case, but when the troops arrive they will find Utah a desert. Every house will be burned to the ground, every tree cut down and every field laid waste.' "

The following Sunday, Captain Van Vliet attended services in the Tabernacle, and when Elder Taylor asked those present (about 4,000) if they were willing to do this, every hand in the audience was raised. The Captain said that he was sure Utah had been misrepresented and that he would hurry back to Washington to use his influence in favor of the Territory.

To this Father replied, "I believe that God sent you here and that good will grow out of it. I was glad when I heard you were coming. If we can keep peace for this winter, I feel sure that something will occur to save the shedding of blood."

During his visit he was introduced to Father's wives and children and was taken through our orchards and gardens. It is reported that when he asked one woman if she would destroy her home for religion's sake, she replied that not only would she do so but that she would stay up nights to do it.

In the meantime, Washington was very far away, the army was close at hand, and drastic steps needed to be taken.

On the fifteenth of September, Father pro-

claimed Utah under martial law. He forbade all
armed forces to enter the Territory and directed
the militia to hold itself in readiness to repel any
attempt at invasion. In spite of the fact that the
army was on the way avowedly to install a new
executive, Father took the position that he was
"still the governor" and therefore had the authority to forbid the entrance of an armed force.

On September 30 an express arrived saying that
the troops were near Fort Bridger, and the soldiers
of the Nauvoo Legion made ready to march under
the direction of General Daniel H. Wells. The
Legion then numbered over six thousand men, and
instructions had already been sent out to make
every needful preparation for a winter campaign.

From the very earliest days of the Church it
had been necessary for its members to be on the
defensive, and the Legion had first been organized
back in Nauvoo, Illinois, with the Prophet Joseph
Smith as its commander. Upon his death Father
succeeded to the command but resigned after
reaching the valley when Daniel H. Wells became
Lieutenant-General and brought its numbers up
to thirteen thousand men, well armed, well drilled,
and highly proficient.

It was with part of these forces that General
Wells prepared to hold back the armies of the
United States, but under Father's strict orders,
"without the shedding of one drop of blood." The
General made his headquarters at Echo Canyon
with a force of 1,250 men. Here he directed Gen-

eral N. V. Jones to have his men dig trenches and make dams across the canyon so that it might be flooded and to pile rocks and boulders upon the mountainsides to be used against the troops in case they attempted to force their way through the narrow canyon. The position held by our men there would have enabled them to hold back an army of almost any size.

General Wells then went on to Fort Bridger, where he met Colonel Burton, who had been all this time in the field keeping close track of every movement of the army. From there he sent a copy of Father's proclamation on to Colonel Alexander, who was in charge of the U. S. forces pending the arrival of General Johnston. He was told that the militia was in the field to carry out the instructions of the governor and that they must either retire from the Territory or disarm their forces. The commander paid no attention to these demands other than to reply that he would submit them to General Johnston upon his arrival from the East.

The method of campaign, as outlined by our leaders, was to harass the enemy in every way, in the hopes that it would become impossible for them to remain in the West. General Wells's instructions to Major Taylor, in charge of one of the advance units, were, "On ascertaining the locality of the troops, proceed at once to annoy them in every possible way. Use every exertion to stampede their animals and set fire to their trains. Burn the whole country before them and on their flanks. Keep them from sleeping by night surprises; blockade the road by felling trees or destroying river fords where you can. Watch for opportunities to set fire to the grass on their windward so as if possible to envelop their train. Leave no grass before them that can be burned. *Take no life* but destroy their trains."

Lot Smith was ordered to meet the supply trains and either turn them back or burn them. The first train he met turned back without much argument, although he had no way of knowing, of course, just how far back they would go. He decided to attack the next train after nightfall, in the hopes that many of the teamsters would be drunk and therefore unable to offer a great deal of resistance. With about twenty men, he rode up to the campfires of the enemy but found, to his surprise and discomfiture, that there were two trains, instead of the one he had reckoned on, and probably sixty or seventy men against his twenty. He was facing the firelight, and upon looking back at his force behind him in the darkness he decided that there was no way of knowing whether he had twenty men or a hundred, so he boldly commanded the teamsters to stack their arms.

They obeyed without much hesitation, and then they were given the privilege of taking enough wagons and supplies to get them safely back to their starting point. While the wagons were burning an Indian arrived upon the scene and asked for some presents. He was made very happy with two wagon covers, some soap, and flour. Another train was burned the following day, after the leaders had refused the alternative of turning back.

After a few weeks of this guerrilla warfare Colonel Alexander sent an express to Father threatening extermination if the Mormons continued to resist and emphasizing his confidence in his ability to carry out the orders of the Government. Father wrote back asking him why he had spent an entire month on Ham's Fork if he had such confidence in his ability and also justifying the mode by which the Mormons were defending their homes. He offered to assist the troops to reach Fort Hall or retire within reach of their supplies from the East. He also invited the Colonel and his officers to visit Salt Lake City, provided they left their troops behind them, and promised them safe and courteous treatment within the city.

Colonel Alexander did not avail himself of Father's hospitality, but it so happened that his pet white mule did—although not at all by design. The mule fell into the hands of some of our soldiers and was turned over to Father's care. He received the kindest of treatment and became the subject of considerable diplomatic correspondence. Before he could be returned, however, he died either of grief or of old age and was sincerely mourned by all of the Youngs as well as by his former comrades.

General Johnston joined his troops on the first of November, and they started from Camp Winfield to Fort Bridger, a distance of thirty-five miles. It took them fifteen days to cover this short distance, and they suffered frightfully on the way. The weather was much colder than they had expected to endure—particularly if they had been in Salt Lake Valley, according to plan—and many of their supplies had been burned. Upwards of fifteen hundred head of cattle had been driven off, and many of the remaining herds, as well as horses and mules, froze to death in the bitter cold of the Wyoming mountains. When they reached Fort Bridger they found that it also had been burned by the Utah Militia, so they used the ruins of the fort to store their supplies and made winter quarters on Black's Fork.

General Albert Sidney Johnston was a brave and brilliant soldier who had often been mentioned as the next Commander in Chief of the United States Army. It was thought in some quarters that he had been sent West purely as a political move by those who wished him far distant from the national scene.

The soldiers suffered great privation during the winter, flour being extremely scarce and vegetables and salt lacking entirely. Learning of their sad straits, Father sent a load of salt to Colonel Johnston. The Colonel returned it with every expression of bitterness, but the soldiers, who had wearied of eating poor meat without any salt, salvaged the load and returned it indirectly to camp. Later they were supplied with salt by the Indians at exorbitant prices.

As soon as it was learned at Church headquarters that Johnston did not intend to carry on a winter campaign, all interference on the part of the Utah Militia was forbidden. Some Federal soldiers, who had been captured, were ordered released, and the greater part of the Legion returned to their homes. Only fifty men were left to guard the pass in Echo Canyon.

On the arrival of the Legion in Salt Lake City they were greeted by the citizens with a song that had been written for the occasion by Aunt Eliza R. Snow:

> Strong is the power of Brigham's God,
> Your name's a terror to our foes,
> Ye were a barrier strong and broad
> As our high mountains crowned with snows.
> Then welcome! sons of light and truth,
> Heroes alike in age and youth.

Wilford Woodruff said concerning the return of the Legion: "Through all this President Young has been as calm as a summer's day. The army of Zion is now returning to its home with the same spirit of composure and quietude that it carried with it into the mountains. As the men passed, on their return, by President Young, they gave him a quiet salute and went silently to their homes, while President Young gazed upon them with thanksgiving and praise to the God of Israel."

It is a bit surprising that there could have been so much serenity under the circumstances, for the opposition to the army was distinctly rebellion, if not treason, and the consequences to the leaders could have been very serious indeed.

In spite of the fact that an army lay encamped just beyond the boundaries of the Territory with the prospect that it might be joined by other armies in a few months, that every man in the community might be fighting very shortly, and that the present winter might be the last spent by the Saints in the Salt Lake Valley, the winter of 1857-58 is spoken of as one of the gayest ever known in the Territory. New Year's Day was featured by balls and social gatherings in many of the ward halls, chief among them being a large gathering at Ballou's Hall in the 14th Ward. Dramatic companies and literary associations flourished, balls and parties were frequent in both public halls and homes, and "every amusement suitable was a source of profit to the caterer and pleasure and benefit to the patronizers." The meaning behind all this gaiety is summed up in the words of one writer as follows: "There was the great sagacity and remarkable commonsense leadership of Brigham Young seen in all this jubilee. He was preparing to make his second exodus, if necessary, and did not intend to play his Moses to a dispirited Israel."

After Van Vliet's report at the nation's capitol, President Buchanan found himself in rather an embarrassing position. The expedition was costing several hundred lives, several millions of dollars, was accomplishing practically nothing, and there was no reasonable explanation for having inaugurated it.

In the meantime, the Church authorities were seeking desperately to have the situation cleared at Washington before the return of mild weather should bring additional troops to Camp Scott. There was one man in the East in whom Father had the greatest confidence, and to him, Colonel Thomas L. Kane, was sent a special messenger entreating him to use his influence with the President in behalf of the Mormons.

Although Colonel Kane was in poor health at the time, he hurried to the capitol and offered his services as mediator in this strange conflict. By this time, President Buchanan was being subjected to a great deal of criticism, both at home and abroad, and he was only too happy to seize upon some means whereby he could ease himself out of the situation without too much loss of dignity. He quickly accepted Kane as his emissary, and the Colonel sailed from New York on the fifth of January, arriving in Salt Lake City, by way of California, late in February.

He was joyfully received by the leaders here, and after a few days' rest and discussion of the problems in hand, he proceeded on to confer with Governor Cumming at Camp Scott. This entailed another journey of 113 miles through deep snow, but the gallant Colonel undertook it willingly and after an arduous journey finally reached the lines of the Federal army.

Here he sought out Governor Cumming at once and delivered Father's message to him which was that the Mormons were willing to receive the newly appointed governor and his fellow officials and give them a loyal welcome, if they would come into the valley without the army. But they were not willing that the troops should enter their capital nor be quartered in any city or settlement of of the Territory.

Governor Cumming was willing to accept this proposition readily and proceed at once on to the Territory without the fanfare of an army, but Commander Johnston saw the matter in a different light. He had been sent out to install a governor and he had every intention of doing so, as well as retrieving some of the losses he had suffered and tasting some sweet revenge. He warned Cumming that the Mormons were merely trying to get him in their power, but the governor was more anxious for peace than for martial triumphs and left for Utah accompanied by Colonel Kane and two servants.

The historian Tullidge says of his meeting with Father: "As soon as he (Cumming) had passed the Federal lines he was met by an escort of the Mormon militia and was welcomed as governor of the Territory with military honors. On the 12th of April they entered Salt Lake City in good health and spirits accompanied by the mayor, marshall and aldermen and many other distinguished citizens."

Arrived at the residence of Elder Staines, Governor Young promptly and frankly called upon his successor at the earliest possible moment, and they were introduced to each other by Colonel Kane.

"Governor Cumming, I am glad to meet you," observed Brigham with unostentatious dignity and that quiet heartiness peculiar to him.

"Governor Young, I am glad to meet you, sir," responded His Excellency warmly, at once impressed by the presence and spirit of the remarkable man before him.

"Well, Governor," said Elder Staines, after the interview was ended, "what do you think of President Young? Does he appear to you a tyrant, as represented?"

"No, sir! No tyrant ever had a head on his shoulders like Mr. Young. He is naturally a good man. I doubt whether many of your people sufficiently appreciate him as a leader."

Governor Cumming thought that the entire affair was now a closed matter and that with his acceptance as governor, peace had been restored, but he soon learned that he had not counted sufficiently upon the resolve of this people. As soon as it was known that the troops were to be quartered in the Territory, thirty thousand people abandoned their homes and started on the historic "move south." Their destination was unknown to any save the leaders. They piled a few provisions into their wagon boxes, tied the family cow on behind, and became wanderers once more. Only enough men remained in the city to apply the torches should the soldiers deviate one foot from their lines of march through the city streets.

The governor was appalled at this calm desertion of the fruits of ten years' labor and pled with the people to remain, promising them that no harm should come to them from the army. But this people had met both promises and enemies before and they had no good reason for putting their faith in either. In his report to the Secretary of State he wrote: "The people are moving from every settlement in the northern part of the Territory. The roads are everywhere filled with wagons loaded with provisions and household furniture, the women and children often without shoes or hats, driving their flocks they know not where. Young, Kimball and the influential men have left their mansions without apparent regret, to lengthen the long train of wanderers. The masses announce to me that the torch will be applied to every house indiscriminately throughout the country as soon as the troops attempt to cross the mountains. I shall follow these people and try to rally them."

During May the governor returned to Camp Scott for his wife, and when he brought her back to the deserted city she was so affected that she burst into tears, begged her husband not to allow the army to stay in the city and to do something to bring the Mormons back.

The kind-hearted old governor assured her that he would do all in his power, but he found that his power was of small instance in this matter, for the Saints went steadily on, some stopping at Provo to wait for further developments and others continuing on as far south as Parowan.

It has been said that this exodus was a move of supreme strategy on Father's part. He believed that the spectacle of thirty thousand people leaving their homes with an army at their backs, with no more valid reason for being there than this particular army had, would incite public opinion in their favor as nothing else would, and the potent voice of the press soon proved that he was right. The New York *Times* said in part: "When people abandon their homes to plunge with women and children into a wilderness to seek new settlements, they know not where, they give a higher proof of courage than if they fought for them." And from the other side of the water came a statement of similar nature from the London *Times* which included this statement: "Does it not seem incredible that, at the very moment when the marine of Great Britain and the United States are jointly engaged in the grandest scientific experiments that the world has yet seen, 30,000 or 40,000 natives of these countries, many of them of industrious and temperate habits, should be the victims of such arrant imposition?"

Early in June, Father and others of the Church leaders were called back to the city to meet a

peace commission which had been sent out by
President Buchanan to offer a full pardon for
treason and other crimes and a pledge that the
army should not molest the Saints in any way
by coming into the valley. The Church leaders
received the pardon in rather an ironical frame
of mind, since they had never acknowledged that
they had been guilty of treason nor entered a
plea for pardon. Said Father: "As far as I am
concerned, I thank President Buchanan for for-
giving me, but I really cannot tell what I have
done. I know one thing, and that is that the people called Mormons are a loyal and a law-abiding
people, and have ever been. Neither President
Buchanan nor any one else can contradict that
statement. It is true Lot Smith burned some wagons containing government supplies for the army.
This was an overt act, and if it is for this we are
to be pardoned, I accept the pardon."

On the twenty-sixth of June the army came
through the city, unarmed according to the pledge
that had been made to Father, and without making
a stop until they reached the Jordan River, two
miles west of the city. While passing through the
city streets, Colonel Cooke bared his head in honor
of the brave men that he had led in the march of
the Mormon Battalion. They camped at the Jordan for three days and then went south some
thirty-six miles to Cedar Valley, where they founded Camp Floyd.

During their stay at Provo and elsewhere the

refugees lived in their wagon boxes or any sort
of temporary shelter that could be devised. Some
of them built cane houses on the Provo Bottoms,
and the more fortunate ones were taken into the
homes of friends or relatives. It was during this
"move south" that my future husband, John D.
Spencer, was born.

Early in July, when it became evident that the
army intended to keep pretty much to themselves
in Camp Floyd, the people began moving back to
their homes. Some had planted crops before they
left and had gone back and forth to take care of
them, but the great majority had not troubled to
put in crops about which there was so much un-
certainty as to whether or not they would ever be
harvested, and so, of course, they were very anxious to return and provide against the coming
winter as best they could.

In the long run the coming of the army proved
to be a Godsend to the people of Utah rather than
a disaster. A great many of their supplies were
purchased in the Territory, and such commodities
as butter and eggs brought very high prices. Many
merchants of the city could date their rise to prosperity with the coming of the army in '58.

When the army was called back east to fight on
the side of the Union in the Civil War, goods that
had been shipped from the East were bought by
the Mormons at a mere fraction of their original
cost. Alexander Majors, who was in charge of
the freighting to the Territory, says in his mem-

oirs "that it was necessary to increase the transportation from 400 wagons to 3,500 wagons and teams. It required more than 40,000 oxen to draw the supplies and 4000 men were employed."

After the wagons were unloaded they were taken to Salt Lake City and placed as near to each other as they could stand. Here wagons that had originally cost $150 to $175 each were sold for $10 apiece.

Flour that had cost the government $28.40 a sack sold for fifty-two cents, and many other items were sacrificed on a like scale. Father sent a son-in-law, Hiram B. Clawson, to the sale, where at an outlay of approximately four thousand dollars he purchased about $40,000 worth of goods for our families, servants, and dependents. He also bought the safe which had held $80,000 in gold, which the Government had freighted to Camp Floyd by ox team.

Hiram invited the officers to call upon Father before their departure, and a number of them did, presenting him with the flagstaff of the camp as a token of their present feelings of friendship. It was transplanted to the hill just east of our home, where it stood for many years and bore the nation's flag on all important occasions.

Just before the final breaking up of the camp in July, 1861, the soldiers blew up the arsenal, sank some of their arms in deep wells, and threw others into a huge bonfire. Incidentally, many of the guns were recovered from the wells and served to usher in numerous Fourth and Twenty-fourth of July celebrations.

Colonel Johnston and Father never met. The Colonel left the Territory in March of 1860 to join the Confederate forces and died upon the battlefield when he met General Grant at the Battle of Shiloh.

INDIAN FRIENDS AND FOES

One day, during the year of 1905, as I was busy with my usual household duties, there came a knock at the back door and, upon opening the door, I was startled to see a very old, very fat, and very dirty Indian squaw. Realizing at once that she was too old to do me any harm, I asked her what she wanted.

She peered at me for a while without speaking and then asked abruptly, "You Brigham's girl?"

"Yes," I answered, "I am one of Brigham's girls."

Having satisfied herself upon this score, she sat down on the porch, and I left her and went on with my work, knowing that she would talk when she was quite ready and not a minute before. Finally when I went back to find her almost dozing in the sunshine there she ventured, "I know Brigham. I here when first white people come to valley. Brigham good to my people."

By degrees I drew the rest of her story from her in broken English. She had been only a small girl when the first white settlers came to the Salt Lake Valley in 1847, but she distinctly remembered Father and his wife. She was very anxious to know if I was a child of that wife and seemed disappointed when I told her that it was Aunt

Clara who came to the valley that first year and that my own mother did not come until later.

When I asked how she had found me, she replied that she had gone to the tithing office and asked for one of Brigham's girls and that they had sent her to me as I was the nearest one within reach.

She seemed especially anxious to impress upon me the fact that she had known "Brigham's wife" and that she remembered Father's great kindness to the Indians. Where she came from or where she was going, I didn't learn—only that her tribe was passing through the city and she had made a great effort to see me. I gave her some clothing, which she badly needed, and some food for the inevitable flour sack, and she went her way again through a state vastly changed from the one she had known when she first saw the white people enter it sixty years before.

There is no question but what the problem of keeping the Indians from molesting the settlers to any great degree was one of the most tremendous my father encountered in his task of establishing a place of refuge for his people in an isolated country. He was not entirely successful, of course, in making pacifists out of the red men but, had he been less successful, those first struggling settlements might easily have been wiped out. The Indians had ever been resentful of the white invader who came to usurp his hunting and fishing grounds and make his means of livelihood less certain, and the settlers who came by the thousands to take the land of the Great Basin were not more welcome than their predecessors had been on other frontiers.

Fortunately, for a period of about three years after the pioneers first arrived in the valley, the Indians left them in comparative peace. The first real annoyance on the part of the redskins came in the spring of 1850. By that time a number of settlers had left Salt Lake to establish homes in the fertile valley to the south now known as Utah County. They had built the customary fort and were living in it, going out to their fields in the daytime to plant their crops. At first the Indians had given them no trouble, but shortly they began to steal grain, cattle, and horses. Matters kept going from bad to worse, until finally the people scarcely dared leave the fort at all and were virtually in a state of siege.

Word was sent up to Father that they must have relief and have it quickly. This put him in somewhat of a quandary. He knew, of course, that the fort would have to be relieved, but he disliked shedding blood and starting actual warfare between the whites and Indians. Another consideration entered in at this time, also. The people were already asking for statehood and were anxious to do nothing that would offend the Government. Captain Howard Stansbury, of the United States Topographical Engineers, was surveying in the region, and Father asked what he thought of sending an armed force against the marauders. He not only approved sending the force but helped to outfit it.

Accordingly, some fifty men went down and found the enemy, who outnumbered them two to one, ensconced in a deserted log hut. The fighting continued for two days before the Indians were finally driven out, but at the end of that time many of them were killed and the rest promised to behave.

Father realized fully that if the Mormon colonies were to escape the difficulties that had been the lot of other pioneers he would have to pursue a different policy in his dealings with the Indians. The keynote of this policy is expressed in his message to the Utah legislature in 1854 when he said in part:

"I have uniformly pursued a friendly course toward them, feeling convinced that independent of the question of exercising humanity toward so degraded and ignorant a race of people, it was manifestly more economical and less expensive to feed and clothe them than to fight them."

Two years earlier than this he had sent word to the settlers in Fillmore:

"We exhort you to feed and clothe them so far as it lies in your power, never turn them away hungry from your door, teach them the arts of husbandry, bear with them in all patience and long suffering, and never consider their lives as equivalent for petty stealing."

As may be supposed, the Indians were quick to take advantage of this policy and soon began a practice of begging from door to door, which did not cease for many a year. At that, however, the Saints were glad to give, even to an unreasonable degree, rather than put up with constant stealing and depredations.

As a second part of his Indian policy, Father attempted to establish missions among the "red brethren" in order to educate them and teach them some rudiments of agriculture. The first mission was founded at Harmony, in southern Utah. Twelve men were sent to this distant place in May, 1854, and after what must have been a very weary journey wrote back that they arrived, "enjoying good health, union and peace." They set to work immediately after their arrival planting wheat and digging the inevitable ditches for irrigation. By this means they hoped to be able to help feed the Indians, and they knew that if they fed them, the Indians would willingly stay around to be taught and preached to. The missionaries attempted to clothe them as well, and after giving out what clothing they had brought with them for the purpose, promptly sent back to Salt Lake for more "old clothing, especially shirts, to help cover the nakedness of the Indians, especially the women."

The most famous of the Mormon Indian missionaries was Jacob Hamblin, who was appointed president of the Santa Clara Mission in 1857 and spent the next twenty years of his life in the service of the savage. He was their wise counselor and their true and devoted friend. He understood them, and they learned to love and understand him. Many rifts were averted through the efforts of this courageous and unselfish man.

One of the best known of the interpreters was Dimick B. Huntington, a brother of one of Father's wives, Zina D. Huntington. The Church voted in 1849 that he and Alexander Williams "should have the privilege of trading with the Indians for the community and that all other persons should be prohibited under fine." This plan was adhered to, with only minor violations, for a number of years and helped to curb the dangerous practice of trading firearms and whisky where they could do the most harm.

Father was especially anxious that the Indians be taught how to raise crops and care for livestock in order to compensate them for the loss of their lands. On one occasion he said:

"Let the millions of acres of land now lying waste be given to the Indian for cultivation and use. Let the poor Indians be taught the arts of civilization and to draw their sustenance from the ample and sure resources of Mother Earth, and to follow the peaceful avocations of the tillers of the soil, raising grain and stock for subsistance, instead of pursuing the uncertain chances of war and game for a livelihood."

Of course he was only indifferently successful

in making agriculturists out of the Indian, but
for that matter, no one else has ever been much
more successful.

In spite of this earnest effort to make and maintain peace with the Indian, it was necessary to
be on constant guard against molestation. The
first building in any settlement was the fort, en-
closing the houses and providing safety for the
livestock. The brush was kept clear from the immediate vicinity of the fort, and an ample supply
of arms and ammunition was always kept on hand.

The first house to be built outside of the fort
in Salt Lake City was the home of Father's
brother, Lorenzo D. Young. It was built in the
fall of 1847, just two or three months after the
arrival of the first company of pioneers, and stood
upon the present site of the Beehive House.

The Youngs moved into this small dwelling—
about one-half mile away from the protection of
the fort—very much against the advice and wishes
of their friends, and it so happened that the catastrophe predicted for them was almost realized.
While Uncle Lorenzo was working away from the
house one day, leaving his wife and young baby
alone, a tall Indian appeared and demanded bread.
The mother had only three small biscuits in the
house, and of these she gave the savage two. He
was not satisfied and demanded more. She gave
him the last one, but he still insisted upon more.
She told him that she had no more, whereupon he
became furious and, fitting an arrow to his bow,

took aim at her heart. This pioneer woman was not only courageous—she was also resourceful. Making as if she were going to comply with his demand, she went into the next room and untied a large mastiff. "Seize him," she called in a low voice, and with a bound the dog had sprung at the Indian's throat and thrown him to the floor.

The Indian pleaded for his life, and after taking the precaution to remove his bow and arrow, she called off the dog. The Indian was badly hurt, and Aunt Harriet, matching her courage with kindness, bathed and dressed the wound and sent him away, a sadder and wiser Indian.

The population of Salt Lake City soon grew to be large enough that the Indians failed to be much of a menace inside the city limits, although when the men went to the canyons for fuel or worked in the outlying fields, they always took the precaution to be well armed. When the nine-foot wall was built around the Lion and Beehive Houses in the middle sixties, one reason for its erection was to afford protection against Indians, although I am sure that this must have been a very minor one.

But if the Indians didn't come to fight, they very often came to beg or steal, and throughout my entire childhood the Indian, in his gaily colored trappings, was a very common sight on the streets of the city. One day a squaw came to the Beehive House begging for sugar. They frequently asked for sugar as they had so little sweet—

but for that matter, so did we. This particular
squaw kept staring and staring at Mother's face,
after muttering the usual request. Mother returned the stare in some curiosity and finally
asked her what was the matter. Pointing to her
mouth, the squaw said, "You take 'em out." She
had been smart enough to detect that mother wore
false teeth and wanted to have a look at them.

Before the birth of one of mother's children she
dreamed that a very fine-looking Indian came to
the house. She was so impressed with his appearance that she asked him his name, which he gave
as "Arta de Crista," and when the new baby arrived he was promptly christened 'Arta de Crista"
after the Indian in the dream.

Mother was sitting in the weaving room one
day working at her great spinning wheel when
this same Arta, who was a mischievous fellow,
came up behind her and gave an Indian war whoop
in a loud and intensely realistic fashion. In terror,
Mother knocked the wheel over with one hand
and Arta de Crista over with the other. In addition he received a whole-hearted spanking and
promised never to play Indian again—with Mother as the victim.

As the Indians became less troublesome in Salt
Lake City they seemed to grow more so in the
smaller settlements. By 1865 the Government had
sent an Agent, Colonel Irish, to take charge of
Indian affairs, and he attempted, with Father's
help, to have them sign a treaty which would put

an end to difficulties between the settlers and the Indians.

By the terms of the treaty they were to move over into the Uintah Valley and give up title to the lands they were occupying at that time. They were to be peaceful and not go to war with other tribes except in self-defense. And they were not to molest the whites. In return for giving up the lands they were occupying at that time, the governor was to extend protection to them, farms were to be laid out, grist and lumber mills built, and several thousands of dollars paid to the tribes each year. The Indians were to hunt, fish, and gather berries on all unoccupied lands. Kanosh was the only chief present at the signing of the treaty who was able to attach his own signature to the document, an achievement of which he was very proud. The other chiefs had to be content with attaching their marks.

In his journal, Wilford Woodruff tells the story of the signing of the treaty somewhat as follows: "President Young and company drove to the Indian farm and held a meeting with the Indians. Colonel Irish, the agent, had called upon President Young to assist him in making a treaty, which he had been unable to bring about because of the opposition of the Indians. They stoutly maintained that they didn't want to sell their lands and go away. Mr. Irish made a speech and the Indians made speeches. Then President Young talked to them and explained that it would be best for them to sign the treaty and told them of the advantages that would come to them if they did so.

"They finally said that they would probably do as he said, but they wanted to think it over until the next day. When they met again all the chiefs came forward and signed the treaty, except Sanpitch, who, according to his own claims, was the main chief. Sanpitch was on his dignity and lay on his face in his tent for two whole days. The other chiefs paid no attention to him, as was their custom, and after the affair was all over and the others had received their presents from the whites, Sanpitch came forward and wanted to receive his presents, as well as sign the treaty. He received some presents but they made him come to Salt Lake before they would allow him to sign."

Colonel Johns of the United States Army was present at the time, and Colonel Irish informed him that he "could do nothing with the Indians except through the influence of President Young."

This treaty did not end Indian troubles in the Territory by any means, and during the years of '66 and '67 there were so many depredations in Sanpete and Sevier Counties that it was necessary to keep armed guards on hand all the time that the crops were being harvested. At one time, in Sanpete County, Father directed the millers to give the Indians what wheat they needed and to grind it for them. The Indians received fifty bushels of wheat valued at two dollars a bushel, but, at that, the grain was cheaper than powder and lead.

This persistent policy of feeding the Indians rather than fighting them bore fruit in many instances, one of which was related by a man who was passing through Utah on his way to California. He writes: "I now told the boys that we were in a position where we were dependent on some one and that I had seen enough to convince me that the Indians were perfectly friendly with the Mormons and that for our own benefit, we had better pass ourselves off for Mormons. So we put our right hands to our breasts and said, 'Mormonee' with a cheerful countenance, and that act conveyed to them the belief that we were chosen disciples of the great and only Brigham Young and we became friends at once as all acknowledged. The fine looking Indian, who sat as King in the lodge made himself known as Chief Walker and, when I knew this, I took great pains to cultivate his acquaintance."

One of the first acts of the Assembly of the State of Deseret in 1850 was a measure designed to stop the traffic in Indian children. Trading parties from New Mexico would come up yearly with horses, guns, and ammunition to be exchanged for Indian women and children, who were later sold into slavery. For this reason the Assembly legalized the adoption or apprenticeship of Indian children, the law providing that the child was to be fed, clothed, and educated, and

that the period of indenture was not to exceed
twenty years. The law proved to be quite effective
in stopping the traffic in children.

Often children who had been stolen from other
tribes were left to starve to death unless they
could eke out some sort of miserable existence by
eating roots pulled from the ground. For a time
Father advised the settlers to buy these children
in order to save them from starvation, but the
Indians began to make a racket out of it, and it
had to be stopped.

In many instances, however, kind-hearted settlers continued to take them rather than see them
starved or killed, and there was a time when a
great number of these children were living in
Mormon homes. One woman bought a ten-month-
old girl for a quilt and a shirt. She reared the
child as a sister to her own children, and when
the girl was grown she married a white man and
reared a large family of her own.

One such girl—Sally—became a member of our
own household and lived with us for many years
until romance finally took her back to her own
people. When only a child, Sally and another girl
had been captured by a tribe, who were enemies
of her own people, and cruelly mistreated. The
other girl died, but Sally was bought by a brother
of Aunt Clara Decker and given to her to be cared
for.

At first Sally was taciturn and unresponsive and
cared little for such mundane duties as darning

stockings and sewing carpet rags, but Aunt Clara
eventually won her over and had made a wonderful housekeeper out of her by the time she was
grown. Needless to say, she learned to adore Aunt
Clara, who mothered her just as she did her very
own.

By and by Chief Kanosh came courting Sally
and used to do his wooing out in the kitchen, which
was an atmosphere quite far removed from "the
light of the silvery moon" where Indian romances
are supposed to bloom according to song and story.
Sally was not easily won, for by now she was quite
thoroughly converted to the ways of civilization
and had no great yearning to return to the campfire and wigwam, but in time she married Kanosh
and went back with him to his tribe.

Some of the Mormons built her a nice little
cottage where she had real doors and windows,
six chairs, a high post bedstead in the corner, and
plates and dishes in a press. She had her own
cows and made butter, her poultry, eggs, and vegetables, and her lord and master was sent forth
proudly in a clean shirt and collar every Sunday.

Kanosh had already been thrice married before
he ever wooed Sally, which may have prejudiced
her some against him. His first wife was Ann, a
very good woman, who died when her first child
was born. His second was Betsykin, a camp fol-
lower from Camp Floyd, and shortly after this
marriage he took another wife in the person of
Mary Huish, a young Indian girl who had been

reared by a white family in Payson. It is said that he bought Mary for a pony.

Kanosh was very proud of Mary, but Betsykin was intensely jealous of the girl and her white ways. One day when the two women were out in the hills trying to catch squirrels, Betsykin cut the younger woman's throat, threw the body in the bottom of a wash, and covered it with oak brush.

The body was not found for a long time, but when it was finally located, Betsykin confessed and had to atone for her crime by starving herself to death. She went out into the hills to a lone wickiup, and when her beacon light was seen burning no more the watchers knew that she had paid the penalty and they burned the wickiup.

Sally tried her best to make Kanosh live in the fashion of the white men, but eventually had to give it up as a bad job, although she never fully reverted to Indian ways herself. He would use the little house only upon state occasions, and at one time, to gratify him, Father paid him a visit there.

He was on one of his journeys south and stopped the carriage in front of the door, expecting Kanosh to come out and greet him. Seemingly no notice was taken of his arrival, and when he sent a messenger in to announce him, Kanosh sent back answer that when he went to see "Bigham, Bigham sat still in his house; and what was manners for Bigham was manners for Kanosh."

"He's right," was Father's reply, and, leaving his carriage, he went in to pay his respects to the chief.

He found Kanosh seated like Solomon in all his glory, cross-legged in the middle of the four-poster bed. He wore a heavy overcoat buttoned to the chin, a pair of new boots, and a gorgeous red blanket over all. And this in spite of the fact that it was a very warm day in May.

Kanosh sat erect and motionless in all his dignity, and Father attempted to maintain at least a comparative dignity, but his efforts were completely upset when one of the wives cautiously raised her head from beneath the bed to gain first-hand knowledge of her lord's appearance. Father was forced to indulge in laughter long and loud.

By far the most troublesome of the Indian chiefs was Walker, who always pretended a great friendship for Father and the Mormons, but who seldom lost an opportunity for causing them grief if he could discover one. It must be said, however, that Walker was usually more venomous in his dealing with enemy Indian tribes than he was with the whites.

Gwinn Harris Heap, the superintendent of Indian affairs in California, wrote of him in 1854: "The Utah chieftain is a man of great subtlety and indomitable energy. He is not a Utahn by birth, but has acquired such an extraordinary ascendency over that tribe by his daring exploits that all the restless spirits and ambitious young

warriors in it have joined his standard. Having
an unlimited supply of fine horses and being in-
nured to every fatigue and privation, he keeps
the territories of New Mexico and Utah, the prov-
inces of Chihuahua and Sonora and the southern
portion of California, in constant alarm. His
movements are so rapid and his plans so secretly
laid, that he has never once failed in any enterprise, and has scarcely disappeared from one dis-
trict before he is heard of in another. He frequently divides his men into two or more bands,
which, making their appearance at different points
at the same time, each headed, it is given out, by
the dreaded Walker in person, has given him with
the ignorant Mexicans, the attribute of ubiquity.
The principal object of his forays is to drive off
horses and cattle."

One of Father's first contacts with the chief was
on an occasion when he was returning from a visit
to some of the settlements of southern Utah. There
were thirty wagons in the party, so they felt themselves reasonably safe from molestation by the
Indians, but at that, they were not too well pleased
to be met by a band of Walker's men brandishing
bows and arrows and filling the air with their
fiendish yells. Father learned that Walker was
camped a few miles away and thereupon drove
his wagons directly into the middle of the camp
and settled down for the night. It happened that
there was a sick child among the Indians whom
the medicine man had given up to die, and Walker

made the very simple request of having a white man to share its death and accompany it on the journey. Instead, Father went and prayed and administered to the child, who shortly recovered. It was this act which first won Walker's friendship for Father—such as it was.

Not long after this the Indians became very troublesome around the vicinity of Paragonah. There were so few people in this little settlement that Father considered it unsafe for them to remain there longer and advised them to move four miles south to Parowan. Such a move meant the complete destruction of all their previous labor in the making of homes, the houses all being demolished so that doors, windows, and everything else portable could be taken on the wagons for a future dwelling place.

When Walker heard of the move he replied with the greatest insolence that "the Mormons were d—d fools for abandoning their houses and town for he did not intend to molest them there, as it was his intention to confine his depredations to their cattle, and that he advised them to return and mind their crops, for, if they neglected them, they would starve and be obliged to leave the country, which was not what he desired, for then there would be no cattle for him to take."

The greatest parley that ever took place between the Mormons and the Indians was during the middle fifties, when nearly one hundred wagonloads of Church authorities and their families went down to Walker's permanent camp to meet with him and other leading chiefs. Often on a cold winter night, as we gathered around the great Franklin stove, Father would relate the details of his meeting with these once famous Indians, and in the shadowy corners of the room I could almost see for myself the tall, majestic forms of Walker, Arapeen, and Peteetneet.

Father had made great preparations for this treaty, because he hoped that it would be the means of establishing permanent peace between the two peoples. Accompanying him from Salt Lake City were such Church leaders as Heber C. Kimball, Wilford Woodruff, John Taylor, Ezra T. Benson, his brother Lorenzo Young, Erastus Snow, and Parley P. Pratt and a number of the other brethren as well as numerous of their wives and children. Besides those who traveled in wagons, there were fifty young men mounted on horses. Altogether they must have made a most impressive cavalcade as they journeyed down through the valleys to the Sevier River. At least it was designed to impress the Indians.

When the company arrived at a place in the vicinity of Walker's camp, Father sent a messenger to inform the chief that he would be ready to give him an audience at a certain hour that day. He had mistaken his man, however. Walker was not receiving an audience—he was giving one—and the word came back that "if Governor Young wanted to see him, he must come to him at his camp, as he did not intend to leave it to see anybody."

Father was somewhat concerned about this attitude and began to wonder if perhaps Walker had changed his mind and decided not to make a treaty after all, but it was merely the Indian's cunning in pretending a great indifference about the whole affair. However, Father gave word that the entire company was to proceed to Walker's camp, which they did, and were met by a number of chiefs including Kanosh, Ammon, Peteetneet, Squash-Head, Grosepine, and others.

Walker's lodge was in the center of the camp, and Father, with some of his aids, was invited to go inside. He found Walker sitting in solemn dignity upon his buffalo robe, wrapped in his blanket, and surrounded by a guard of honor composed of old chiefs. He did not rise, but held out his hand to Father and invited him to sit down at his side.

At this point everybody shook hands all around, after which they proceeded with the more serious business of the day. Dimick Huntington acted as interpreter and made a long speech in which he said that the Mormons had come in the hopes of smoking the pipe of peace and ending all hostilities on either side.

For a time there was no further speaking from either side until finally an old grey-haired chief got up and, stretching his withered, battle-scarred arms aloft, said:

"I am for war. I never will lay down my rifle and tomahawk. Americats have no truth—Americats kill Indian plenty—Americats see Indian woman, he shoot her like deer—Americats no meet Indian to fight, he have no mercy. One year gone, Mormon say they no more kill Indian—Mormon no tell truth. Plenty Utahs gone to great Spirit, Mormon kill them—no friend to Americats more."

He was followed by the chief of the Sanpete Indians who likewise was full of grievances against the whites and saw no very good reason for attempting to maintain peace with them.

Other chiefs rose in their turn, standing in stern dignity with their blankets held close about them as they talked either for peace or for continued warfare.

Finally Father asked Walker to talk, but he shook his head saying, "No, I got no heart to speak. Tonight Wakara talk with Great Spirit, tomorrow Wakara talk with Governor."

The pipe of peace was then handed around the entire circle with each one present taking one or two whiffs, and the council was over.

The following morning all were assembled once more in Walker's lodge, and Father spoke to them as follows:

"I love the Indian like a father and I want to be friends with all of them. I will give them plenty of clothing and good food if they will be friends with the white man and not fight and kill any more. I have brought many presents with me for the Indian—clothing, blankets, rifles, ammunition and oxen." At this point he ordered the sixteen head of oxen, which he had brought along, driven into the camp, and the sight of them made the chiefs show much warmer feelings than heretofore.

Then for the first time, Walker expressed himself: "Wakara has heard all of the talk of the good Mormon chief. Wakara no like to go to war with him. Sometimes Wakara take his young men, and go far away to sell horses. When he is absent, then Merecats come and kill his wife and children. Why not come and fight when Wakara is at home? Wakara is accused of killing Captain Gunnison. Wakara did not. Wakara was three hundred miles away when the Merecat chief was slain. Merecats soldier hunt Wakara to kill him, but no find him. Wakara hear it; Wakara come home. Why not Merecats take Wakara- He is not armed. Wakara heart very sore. Merecats kill Parvain chief and Parvain woman. Parvain young men watch for Merecats, and kill them, because Great Spirit say—'Merecats kill Indian; Indian kill Merecats.' Wakara no want to fight more. Wakara talk with Great Spirit; Great Spirit say—'Make peace.' Wakara love Mormon chief; he is good man. When Mormon first come to live on Wakara's land, Wakara give him welcome. He give Wakara plenty bread, and clothes to cover his wife and children. Wakara no want to fight Mormon; Mormon chief very good man; he bring plenty oxen to Wakara. Wakara talk last night to Payede, to Kahutah, San Pete, Parvain—all Indian say, "No fight Mormon or Merecats more.' If Indian kĭll white man again, Wakara make Indian howl."

The calumet of peace was again handed around, and all the party took a smoke. The council was then dissolved.

It was not to be expected, however, that Walker would greatly change his ways, no matter how impressively he smoked the pipe of peace, and the whites, as well as enemy tribes, continued to have unpleasant contacts with the great chief. On one Sunday, Father said to his congregation: "How many times have I been asked in the past week what I intend to do with Walker. I say, Let him alone, severely. I have not made war on the Indians nor am I calculating to do it. My policy is to give them presents and be kind to them. Instead of being Walker's enemy, I have sent him a great pile of tobacco to smoke when he is lonely in the mountains. He is now at war with the only friends he has upon this earth and I want him to have some tobacco to smoke."

Walker died in 1855, and Father, not knowing that he was ill, had sent him some letters and presents which reached him only the day before he died. According to his wish, they were buried with him. He expressed great anxiety for peace with the whites as well as the greatest friendliness toward Father and the Mormons. As was befitting for the spiritual journey of so great a chief, two squaws, two Payede children, and fifteen horses were killed to form his retinue to the happy hunting grounds.

The one Indian chief who proved, as well as professed, his friendship was Washakie, chief of the eastern Shoshone band. He was a fine-looking, powerfully built man of commanding and dignified carriage and was known throughout the West as a noble character and a true friend of the white man. His life span extended throughout the entire nineteenth century, as he was born, according to very good authority, in 1798 and died February 20, 1900. Just three years before his death, in 1897, he was baptized a member of the Episcopal Church.

By profession he was a bow and arrow maker, fashioning superior bows from elk horns wrapped with sinews. He was also an expert in their use, although in his later life he used a flintlock rifle. For a number of years he was in the employ of the Hudson's Bay Company as a guide, in which capacity he was especially valuable. He was a great friend of that well-known frontiersman, Jim Bridger, and was always willing to help the emigrants to cross streams, find livestock, or build bridges. In appreciation for these services, nine thousand of them signed a letter at one time commending him for his help.

I think that perhaps the finest tribute ever paid to Father by an Indian was that uttered by Peteetneet, the brother of Walker, when he said, "What the other white men say go in one ear and out the other but what Brigham says goes to the heart and stays there."

SCHOOLS

In 1847 Father stood on the banks of the Missouri River and addressed an assembly of toil-worn pioneers who had paused for a brief respite before making the final great effort that would bring them through the tortuous mountain passes ahead and into a promised land. In the covered wagons that stood near by was space for only the barest necessities to take them through the remainder of their journey and help sustain life until they should gain a foothold in the new country. Many things had been brought thus far that would have to be discarded and, fearful lest they be books, Father said:

"It is desirable that all Saints should improve every opportunity of securing at least a copy of every valuable treatise on education—every book, map, chart or diagram that may contain interesting, useful and attractive matter to gain the attention of children and cause them to learn to read; and also every historical, mathematical, philosophical, geographical, geological, astronomical, scientific, practical and all other variety of useful and interesting writings, maps, etc., to present to the general church recorder, when they shall arrive at their destination, from which important and interesting matter may be gleaned to

compile valuable works on every science and subject for the benefit of the rising generation. We
have a printing press, and any one who can take
good printing or writing paper to the valley will
be blessing themselves and the church. We also
want all kinds of mathematical instruments together with all rare specimens of natural curiosities and works of art that can be gathered."

The Saints heeded his words, and any who could
tucked in an old textbook among the blankets and
sent word back to those who were following to do
the same.

The first school in the valley was opened in
October, about three months after the arrival of
the first companies, and was taught by Mary Jane
Dilworth. The schoolhouse was an old military
tent, shaped round like a wigwam and placed
near the center of the fort. The teacher had the
dignity of an old campstool for a seat, but the
nine pupils had to be contented with logs. The
school was opened with prayer, and the first day
was spent learning a psalm from the Bible and
singing songs. Writing materials were varied and
unique. Some of the pupils had slates and pencils,
and others had pens and paper, but those who had
neither took charcoal and wrote on smooth logs
or dried the bark of the white mountain birch.
When nothing better was available for the mid-
day meal, the children went out and dug sego
roots.

During the following winter, schools were

opened for adults as well as for children, the principal subjects taught being foreign languages for the very good reason that there was always available, as a teacher, some person who had come from another country as a convert or had served as a missionary. One such teacher was Addison Pratt, who had been to the Society Islands and taught the Tahitian language to a class of twenty persons three evenings a week. Other languages which are claimed to have been taught successfully during the winter of '47 were Hebrew, Greek, Latin, and German.

Along with the Tahitian language, the pioneers were also privileged to learn some facts concerning astronomy. Orson Pratt, who was a mathematical genius, gave lectures in astronomy and other scientific subjects in the Council House. His announcement stated that "the admittance to the series would cost $1.20, a single lecture $ .20. Doors open at 6 o'clock with the lecture commencing precisely at half past six."

It was soon after the organization of the provisional government of the State of Deseret that Father, as Governor, signed an act passed by the first legislative assembly incorporating the University of the State of Deseret. Orson Spencer was appointed Chancellor with a board of twelve regents.

A committee was appointed to co-operate with Father in selecting a site for the location of the University, and when he announced that he had chosen a site on the east bench of the city, his decision was immediately accepted. They decided to enclose the grounds with a rock wall, and 135 rods of this wall were actually completed by 1853 with enough stone hauled to build three fourths of a mile more. The city council passed a law designating ground in the vicinity for herding and grazing ground for the animals of the men who should be working on the University.

The University was first called the "Parents' School" and was opened in the home of John Pack in November of 1850, under the direction of Orson Spencer. Dr. Collins was employed as a teacher, and he endeavored to give instruction in all branches of high school learning. The classes of the school were held in the parlor while across the hall was the first mercantile store opened in Utah. The terms were eight dollars for one quarter, but as usual the produce of the valley was taken in lieu of money.

Textbooks were at a premium, in spite of the fact that the emigrant companies had been urged to bring all that they could possibly carry. In '51 Father sent Dr. Bernhisel to New York to purchase a library which was shipped across the plains by ox team. The original cost was five thousand dollars, and of course the shipping added materially to this sum. The books consisted largely of ancient and modern classics. Two large globes were also brought by ox team. One was a map of the world and the other an astronomical map. During the Fourth of July celebration in '69 these globes, mounted on platforms, were hauled in the procession on wagons.

The University classes were later held for a time in the Council House and, by the time I was ready to attend, had moved to what is now an old knitting factory building over on the west side. It was here that I received my diploma signed by Dr. John R. Park.

My school days began in a kindergarten taught by Camilla Cobb, the first such school in the state. Camilla had been brought here from Germany by the eminent educator Karl G. Maeser. The American translation of her German name being quite unusable, she took the name of Maeser until her marriage to one of Aunt Augusta Cobb's sons by a former marriage. When I attended Camilla's kindergarten, it was held in the front room of Aunt Augusta's home on State Street.

All too soon, kindergarten became a thing of the past, and I was sent over to a school on the corner of West South Temple and Richards Streets taught by Milton H. Hardy and Seraph Young, a cousin. I was still very young, and only a few incidents stand out clearly in my memory —among them, that of the button charm. There were very pretty buttons in those days, and it became a craze among the younger generation to make long strings of them. One button on the string was a "charm," and anyone who touched it had to relinquish one of her own buttons.

One day we were marching around the room, and the line of march took us past the teacher's desk. The girl just ahead of me very deftly removed an apple from the desk and slipped it in her pocket. The teacher glanced over just afterward and, seeing that I was still in the vicinity, asked sharply, "Did you take that apple?"

"No," I answered.

"Do you know who took it?"

"Yes," I replied, "but I won't tell."

"Then go and sit in the corner," came the stern pedagogical command.

I didn't propose to suffer the embarrassment of sitting in the corner for so trivial an offense, so I walked over to where the coats and nubias hung, put mine on, and went home. When I arrived there, Father was just having his ten-o'clock breakfast and asked what was the matter. I explained, putting myself in the best light, of course, and more than a little afraid that I would be marched promptly back to school. After a moment's reflection, however, he said, "Well, you can go and sit in a corner here—and play with your buttons." The latter suggestion, I am sure, was designed to keep me amused and insure him peace from my chatter.

I next attended school in our own schoolhouse built just east of the Beehive House. It was here that all of Father's children, together with a few of the neighbors' children, learned the multiplication tables and the various tenses of verbs.

(Photo Courtesy Utah Historical Society)   Brigham Young's School House

Those days were very happy ones, and I remember the old schoolhouse with a great deal of sentiment and affection. There was an entrance vestibule about eight feet square, and from its ceiling hung a bell rope just within reach of a grown person and quite beyond the reach of us very young persons who used to look longingly at its tantalizing length. Each morning the bell would ring at fifteen minutes of nine and again at nine, when it was time for lessons to begin.

As we hurried in from the playground I never failed to glance up at the belfry, for the ringing would send a great flock of doves out over our heads, spreading their wings and giving one a feeling of uplift and happiness. The main schoolroom was large with an eighteen- or twenty-foot ceiling and high windows which gave an excellent light upon our desks. These old-fashioned desks were painted bright green and were made with drop lids which, when raised, were highly convenient for such clandestine acts as eating apples during study period or reading notes from the boys.

The object that would distinguish it most from the modern schoolroom was the large round stove which stood in the center of the room. Yards and yards of black stovepipe stretched away to the chimney corner, and around the middle of the stove was a two-inch ledge where our apples baked throughout the long morning. Towards noon as our stomachs became emptier, these apples sizzled with an almost unbearably tantalizing odor.

During the winter months we would come to school well clothed in warm woolen stockings, nubias, and bright wool comforters. One could always while away a pleasant half-hour when lessons palled by picking bits of highly colored wool from the garments and patting them into designs. The more ingenious of us could fashion them into bookmarks or even Christmas presents of a sort.

Friday was always the one day of the week for which we longed, for on that day all studies and exercises were put aside for the afternoon, and we would have a program of declamations, spelling matches, organ solos, and singing, ending up with the school paper, which was made up entirely of contributions from the scholars. I recently saw one that was written in the early seventies and found that Heber J. Grant, the present head of the Church, and myself were the only surviving contributors.

A visitor from the East* during 1865 wrote of our school: "By Brigham's invitation I spent an hour in his school. Its register bore the names of 34 pupils; three Brigham's grandchildren; all the rest his own sons and daughters. There were 28 present from 4 to 17 years of age, on the whole looking brighter and more intelligent than the children of any other school I ever visited.

* Albert D. Richardson.

"With three of the prophet's daughters I had some conversation. Their language is good and their manners graceful. One has a classic face and another so pretty that half the young men of the church are in love with her."

On the whole, I suppose we were as well behaved as the average set of school children—but most certainly no better, and many a time the monotony of the day was broken by a prank from one of the scholars. There was one lad who didn't even wait for the school day to begin but, arriving very early one morning, climbed up into the belfry and pulled the bell rope after him. He then proceeded to ring the bell loudly and long, awakening many of the townspeople and bringing the teacher to her post in a state of half undress to find out what calamity had befallen. When she discovered that it was only young Robert Pyper venting his repressed desires upon the bell, she began searching for a ladder to bring him down, and when none could be found she had the boys stand upon one another's shoulders so that Robert could be brought down to justice. I personally thought him quite a hero.

Father told all his sons that any of them who wished might go East to college provided they would prepare themselves by first obtaining the best in education that the state had to offer. Another condition was that when they returned to the state they were to disseminate the knowledge they had gained among the young people here.

There were no half measures with Father: the boys either made good at school or they were taken out.

Don Carlos, the only son now living, thought that he preferred to be with the teamsters, so Father immediately took him out of school and put him to work driving a pair of blind mules up to the sawmill in City Creek Canyon to get flooring for the Tabernacle. Carlos didn't like driving the mules either so he went back and finished college and then went to Troy, New York, to the Rensselaer Polytechnic School of Engineering. He entered with five conditions but was graduated and came back to Utah, where he first taught in the Brigham Young University and eventually became Church architect. Altogether, five of the boys went to Eastern universities. Willard W. went to West Point and was an outstanding student there. The New York papers carried stories of the Mormon and the nigger at West Point, and there were actually people who came from the city to see the two curiosities. Willard became a Colonel in the United States Army, was an instructor at West Point for some years, fought in the Spanish-American War, and was head engineer for the locks on the Columbia River.

Alfales studied law at Ann Arbor, and Feramorz, who was my full brother, was graduated from the Naval Academy at Annapolis and later went to Rensselaer with Don Carlos.

THE THEATRE

The most fascinating spot to me in the entire city, outside of my own home, was the great Salt Lake Theatre, spoken of by Henry Miller, many years after it had been built, as a "cathedral in the desert." It was there that I sat wide-eyed and watched beautiful ladies being saved from the clutches of the dark-browed villain in such plays as "Lady Audley's Secret" and "The Lancashire Lass," or gasped in amazement while the Japanese acrobats built their marvelous human pyramid. Not until the very littlest one had reached the top and given his triumphal "Ki-yi," whereupon the pyramid dissolved and each participant leaped lightly to the safety of the floor again, could I breathe a sigh of relief and sit comfortably back in my seat once more.

People were always amazed when they saw, for the first time, this wonderful theatre built in the days when materials had to be hauled across a thousand miles of country by ox teams and wagons. A people less valiant and less determined to have the finer things of life and without the leadership and vision of a man like my father could certainly never have accomplished this huge undertaking. Many a man hauled timbers all day long for its

construction with no better pay than the promise
of future theatre tickets.

Father realized that this people, being almost
completely shut off from contacts with the outside
world, must themselves provide the means for their
cultural uplift and entertainment. He must have
felt that the arduous task was fully justified, for
years after the theatre was built he said, "If I
were placed on a cannibal island and given a task
of civilizing its people, I should straightway build
a theatre for the purpose."

Naturally there were many other supporters of
the drama who helped to pave the way for this
enterprise. Among them was Phil Margetts, a
talented amateur actor who had organized the
Mechanics' Dramatic association and was giving
performances in "Bowring's Theatre," which was
simply Mr. Bowring's home minus, as yet, the
partitions. As Brother Margetts was anxious to
secure Father's favorable support he invited him,
one day, to bring his counselor, Heber C. Kimball,
together with both of their families, to come and
witness a performance. They accepted the invitation, although "bringing their families" meant
that a crowd of slightly less than a hundred must
be accommodated in the tiny building. Father
was very much pleased with the project and at
the end of the play announced that the time was
ripe for the building of a big theatre and made
his statement which has since become famous,

"The people must have amusement as well as religion."

Hiram B. Clawson was among those who had urged such an undertaking, and to him Father entrusted the task of finding a suitable site and securing building materials. Strangely enough, Johnston's army, which had come to Utah with the avowed purpose of making war upon the Mormons, was greatly instrumental in furnishing means and materials for the construction of the playhouse.

The soldiers had been at Camp Floyd, several miles south of the city, for about a year when they were ordered East to take part in the Civil War and were commanded to sell their remaining stock of supplies at auction.

Father sent Hiram B. Clawson to the "sale" with $4,000, and there he bought such things as cook stoves and groceries that later were resold for ten times the amount paid and formed the nucleus for the theatre building fund. Among the most valuable of his purchases were boxes of nails worth $40 which he was able to buy for only $6. Later on, when these nails had all been used and there was no place to buy any more, Father sent teamsters to the Government wagons which had been burned at the approach of the army and had them bring back pieces of iron which were hammered by hand into nails for the construction of the theatre.

Through the united efforts of practically everybody in the community, the building was eventually finished. Talented converts to the Church from England or the Eastern states designed the interior, added artistic decorations, and painted the scenery. The auditorium had a seating capacity of two thousand. It was arranged with a parquet and four circles and was easily the finest building in western America at the time.

It is said that during the winter of 1861 the center of interest with Salt Lake's population alternated between two points—(1) the wall in front of the *Deseret News,* whereon were posted bulletins of the great Civil War then raging and (2) the great building two blocks away, the mammoth "New Theatre."

The building was formally opened in 1862, just two years after my birth, so my very earliest remembrances include this beautiful place. The opening took place before the building was entirely finished, and as there was no heat, Father sent word in his invitations for the people to wear their heavy underwear and rubbers so that they would not feel too much discomfort.

In the address which he gave upon this occasion he said that "every pure enjoyment was from Heaven and was for the Saints and when they came together with pure spirit and with faith that they would pray for the actors and actresses they would be refreshed and benefited in their entertainments and that those on the stage should ever be as humble as if they were preaching the gospel. Truth and virtue must abound and characterize every person engaged on the stage or they should be immediately ejected from the building. No person would be permitted to bring liquor into this edifice." As long as Father lived the characters of the performers were subjected to his most careful scrutiny. At one time when the talented actor George Pauncefoote was playing in the city for a number of weeks, Father purposely stayed away from the performances because he had heard unfavorable reports of the man's mode of living and therefore gave him this public disapproval.

During the early days the receipts at the door were likely to include anything from string sausage to honey in the comb. The notices of the plays proclaimed, "Cash, also Merchandise, Grain and Home Manufacture received at Cash prices in payment for tickets." There is more than one story told of patrons riding up to the door of this elegant playhouse with a chicken under each arm with which to secure admission. Still more unique was the case of the individual who brought a turkey in payment for his ticket and received two spring chickens in change.

The programs announced in big type that "children in arms will not be admitted," this procedure probably being necessary because there was almost always an abundance of young babies in early Utah families. When this notice did not prove entirely effective, it was changed to a blaring, "Babies in arms Ten Dollars each." I never heard of the ten dollars being paid.

Along with the babies, firearms of any description were excluded from the playhouse, and during each evening's performance a collection of pistols, six-shooters, and what not rested in the treasurer's office, each properly identified for return to the owners at the conclusion of the play.

Lighting of the building was accomplished during the first few years with oil lamps, nearly four hundred of them being required for the purpose. On either side of the stage were posts holding kerosene lamps placed one above another, which served to light the stage well, if not brilliantly. The footlights presented rather a difficult problem but were controlled to some degree by a small shaft which ran from lamp to lamp and was turned to right or left as the lighting required. When the first plays were presented the lights were blown out if the stage needed to be darkened and relighted as the scene demanded.

Always near the lamps were kept buckets of sand and barrels of salt water to be used in case of fire, and it was likely to fare ill with the person in charge of these safeguards if Father found that he was neglecting his duties in any way. Often I would go with him down the little staircase direct to the stage, cross over to the big room where the lamps were cleaned, filled, and made ready for use. I can hear him telling Brother Derr to be extremely careful and watchful of the lights at all times. One night when three oil lamps in the footlights caught fire, Father stepped out across the stage and fanned out the flames with his broad-brimmed hat. Such was the people's confidence in him on all occasions that there was not even a suggestion of panic at this time.

It was necessary for the property man to be little short of a genius in order to meet the demands made upon him. The people of the city came to the rescue many a time with their personal belongings, and usually the plays were produced with all the essentials. Among the properties were a number of guns for use of the chorus in the opera seasons. They were all flintlocks, and many of them carried the name of Harpers Ferry Arsenal for the year 1813. Pioneers who had fought in the war of 1812 had brought their guns along for protection on the plains and then had generously turned them over for use in the theatre.

Charles Millard, the property man at the theatre, had been an apprentice in the same capacity at the Drury Lane Theatre in London. Of his experiences in fashioning properties out of next to nothing, he wrote: "I well remember the first play, 'The Pride of the Market.' The first scene was a market place where vegetables, fish and flowers were needed. How to make them was a problem. At last I saved up every scrap of paper I could find, pasted strip on strip and then made frames of wire or with cardboard and made articles from this. Also made paper maché and fashioned stage properties from this. We then made the goblets with a wooden lathe. The fish we covered with cloth and painted.

"The second scene was a marble parlor and here again we had to use ingenuity. I received permission to borrow properties from President Young's home, which I did, and also used Hiram Clawson's upright piano. The big chairs were President Young's parlor set. We had no carpet, so had to paint a snow white cloth on one side and, having no stencils, did it all by hand. I also painted a table and a cover in the same manner to match the set, which, if I say it myself was a corker. In fact, a traveling company from New York offered $1,000 for the set, which was a pile of money in those days."

There were times when these home-made properties failed to measure entirely up to requirements. One such case on record was that of the cannon used in the production of "The Lonely Man of the Ocean." The sailors were lying about on the ship either dead or dying of yellow fever. The hero and heroine, standing alone on the deck, saw a distant sail and thought to save themselves by touching off the cannon for a signal. The cannon failed to go off, however, and upon the whispered advice of a stage hand the hero touched off the cannon a second time while the stagehand fired a pistol. After the curtain had fallen the cannon came to life and went off, striking two of the sailors and inflicting slight wounds.

The townspeople were always willing to come forth with their treasured possessions if they were needed for the good of the theatre, and there is no more touching example of sacrifice than that of John McDonald, who gave the very hair off his head when occasion, or rather a leading lady, demanded.

During the performance of a play, Sara Alexander was made up as a blonde when the rôle called for a brunette. Father always took a keen interest in even these slight details and pointed the discrepancy out to her. Sara replied that she would dearly love to comply with his wishes in the matter and could very easily do so if she could only have the glossy black curls of John McDonald to adorn her own head. Brother McDonald was inordinately proud of his wonderful locks that reached down to his shoulders, but when Father explained the situation to him, he hesitated only one brief moment and then said gallantly, "If the success of the play depends upon my hair, Brother Brigham, you shall have my hair."

There was one other time when Father was not quite so successful in having the costuming meet his desires. A professional ballet was scheduled to appear, and Father ordered that their skirts must come to their ankles. The manager's idea of what the proper length of a ballet skirt should be differed greatly from Father's; however, on the first night of the appearance of the ballet the girls danced in ankle-length skirts. On each succeeding night for a week the wily manager cut off several inches from the bottoms of the tarlatan skirts until at the final performance they had reached the forbidden knees before Father was at all aware of what had happened.

Before long my own talented sisters began to take minor parts in plays, and there was one auspicious occasion when the older girls of the family, known as the "Big Ten," appeared in a ballet in bespangled blue tarlatan dresses, with their hair carefully curled and their faces rouged ever so slightly. There even came a day when I made my own appearance upon the stage of the great theatre. My half-sister Talula and I were chosen to act as fairies in the lavish production of "Cherry and Fair Star." There was also a ballet of fairies in which several of the other girls participated, but our own part was very special— in our own eyes at least. We were to be enclosed within huge flower buds, and at a psychic moment the buds were to come up through the floor, open up, and Talula and I were to step forth and dance. It was all to be very lovely with Talula and me resplendent in pink dresses, wreaths on our heads, and wands in our hands.

We came up through the floor all right and the buds opened according to schedule, but when I stepped forth onto the lighted stage my wreath fell ignominiously from my brow onto my face. I was deeply chagrined and on the following night declared that absolutely nothing would make me

go to the theatre and run chances of being so hu-
miliated again. Mother persuaded, cajoled, and
finally threatened, all without avail. She tried to
appeal to my better nature by reminding me that
the play would be seriously hampered without me.
Apparently I had no better nature. She threatened to tell Father. Usually this had the desired
effect of bringing me to time, but I still remained
adamant. Finally in desperation Mother said that
if I would only go she would give me her gold
watch. It was a large Swiss watch with an open
face, and I had always admired it so I promptly
accepted the watch and prepared to go to the
theatre. The wreath stayed in its proper place
that night so all went well, and I had the watch
in addition—for the time at least.

One night, a short time later, I was suffering
from a slightly sore throat and asked Mother,
whose room I shared, if she would go down and
get me a drink of water. She answered, "Now,
Clarie, you know that you have always been
taught to wait on yourself. You will have to go
down and get your own drink." I pondered this
over for a moment and then said, "If you will go
down and get me the water, I'll give you back
your gold watch." I don't know whether Mother
wanted very much to regain her watch or whether
she thought I might be in quite serious need of
water, but at any rate she went for the drink and
I gave up the watch. Upon her death it once more

became my prized possession, and I trust that I received it more worthily that time.

The play, "Cherry and Fair Star," marked my last, as well as my first, appearance on the stage of the Salt Lake Theatre, although in later years I assisted in costuming the performances for the Home Dramatic Club and the Opera Company—a rôle for which I had much more talent, I am sure.

As my husband was a prominent member of both companies, I followed their activities with unusual interest and have many pleasant memories of that (to us) golden age of the drama in Utah. They often had engagements in cities other than Salt Lake, and many humorous incidents occurred upon those occasions, two of which I shall relate here. During a performance of the "Chimes of Normandy," John, playing the part of the miser Gaspard, was supposed to put his bags of gold down through a small trap door in the floor. In lieu of a better receptacle a boy stood underneath to receive the bags, but become a trifle overzealous, thrust his hands up in full view of the audience. Kneeling down, John said, "My gold! My gold! My darling gold! My precious gold!" and then in a low voice, but not quite low enough, "Take your hands down, you damn fool." The audience, which had been smiling politely before, now broke forth into pronounced snickering.

At another time John was playing Ko-Ko in "The Mikado" and my nephew, Brigham S. Young, the title rôle. While the company was on the way to

give a performance in Logan, "Bid" left the train
during a stop in Ogden and was in turn left by
the train. Only slightly daunted, he secured a
horse from a livery stable and started out through
a blizzard for the opera house at Logan, fifty
miles away. At various towns along the route, he
attempted to secure a fresh horse, but circumstances were decidedly against him. Antipolyg-
amy raids were in progress, and nothing could
convince the residents that the stranger on the
horse was not a deputy United States marshal
who should be met with locked doors and silence.

Finally at Wellsville, some ten miles away from
his destination, "Bid" helped himself to a mount
tied outside of a drugstore and hastened on to
the opera. He had wired ahead that he was on
the way, and they had stalled along as much as
possible in order to give him time to arrive. Finally as John was singing the number just preceding
the Mikado's entrance he saw "Bid" arrive and
ad libbed until the Mikado could don his gorgeous
robe over his muddy trousers and make his regal
way onto the stage.

Many of these local Thespians received their
first inspiration by being allowed to appear as
"supes" with visiting companies.

One of my brothers' friends, Horace Whitney,
said that his pride knew no bounds when he
marched across the stage with spear and bonnet
as one of the army of Macbeth and then, with the

simple change to battle-ax and helmet, marched back again in the army of Macduff.

On another occasion, when he was cast as an Indian in the play of "Pocahontas," he arrived too late for a wig, but nothing daunted, put on an Indian suit and war paint and joined the band on the stage. His hair was a decidedly sandy shade, and the leading man practically exploded when he saw the unique addition to his cast. As soon as the curtain had been rung down, he called the costumer in and said, "Harry, there may have been blond Indians in the time of Pocahontas but they are now extinct. Get that boy a wig, or send him home." As there was no wig to be had and Horace declined to go home, the costumer took the only other alternative and blackened the offending hair.

The boys were not long content in their rôle of supernumeraries and yearned to do better and more valiant things. Finally they decided to produce their own play. One of their number wrote an ambitious sketch called "The Robbers of the Rocky Mountains," and secured Social Hall for its staging. There was some old scenery stored in our barn, and my brothers generously offered to donate it toward the cause—without first consulting Father, however. The overseer caught them making away with the sets, reported to Father, and they were called to an accounting. Seeing their anxiety over the threatened disaster to the play, Father sent for the manager of the Salt

Lake Theatre and said, "These boys have a play. They call it 'The Robbers of the Rocky Mountains.' I don't know much about the mountains, but they certainly made a clean job of my old barn. Give them a date at the Theatre."

The play was produced on the night of July 13, 1872, before a large audience, which, it must be reluctantly admitted, had come out more because it was the first night on which the theatre was illuminated by gas than to see "The Robbers."

They would have loved to continue upon the boards of the Salt Lake Theatre, but since this was not possible, they determined to carry on and present "Nick of the Woods" in the Widow Gibbs barn. The reasons for selecting the barn were numerous and worthy. It was centrally located, there were a number of old benches lying about in the vicinity, and the rent was negligible—a ball of carpet rags, a flatiron, and a creepy hen being offered to the widow and duly accepted. Besides, there were double doors on the west side which could be thrown open and the illusion of a burning Indian village be created by the setting sun— it was hoped.

There was more than the proverbial fly in the ointment, however. There was a full-grown cow. The Widow Gibbs insisted that the cow be allowed to remain within the barn and, although there was no place for a cow in the plot, stay she did, at least for a time.

The admission was seven pins for the rear part

of the barn, but those who sat in the front two rows and thereby enjoyed a full view of the dressing rooms were assessed one tallow candle in addition. Joe Pitt painted the Indians as Indians had never been painted before, and there was an orchestra composed of a fiddle and an accordion.

In the middle of the overture, the cow broke loose from her assigned place on the stage, came through the curtains, over the benches, and outdoors. The audience didn't miss the cow, but the widow did and sent her small son in with the ultimatum that "the cow couldn't stand out in the rain any longer." It was quite the wrong moment to bring the cow back into the play, especially since there was no place to tie her except to the waterfall (a long board over which Nick was about to descend). Nothing could daunt these ambitious actors, however, and they determined that the play must go on. They ignored the cow and played on until Albert Kimball's mother came after him with a stick for leaving the woodpile. She was not so easily ignored, and the performance came to an abrupt end.

For the first few years the plays were put on almost entirely by a local company led by one or two professional actors who would come from the East for the winter. Naturally there were not many, nor was it often that they would risk their lives coming over the desert by stagecoach, but those who did come among us were very deeply appreciated. Among the brightest of these stars

was the lovely Julia Dean Hayne, who came with
George B. Waldron and others in 1865 and remained to delight Salt Lake audiences through the
next year. Mr. and Mrs. Seldon Irwin, T. A. Lyne,
and Pauncefoote were other popular visitors.
Among the best known of the local players were
Phil Margetts, Nellie Colebrook, Asenath Adams
—the mother of Maude—and Sara Alexander, who
was a ward in my father's home. Asenath, or
Annie, as she was often called, also made her home
with us during the theatrical season, for she lived
some distance from the playhouse and it was inconvenient for her to go back and forth daily in the
wintertime.

Maude Adams' first appearance upon any stage
was on that of the historic old Salt Lake Theatre,
and following is her mother's own version of the
event as related in George D. Pyper's book, *The
Romance of an Old Playhouse:* "We were playing
a double bill—domestic play and 'The Lost Child.'
I had finished in the first play and was standing
in the wings when the maid brought Maude over
to the Theatre to wait for me. Children were
never allowed in the dressing rooms and this appearance of the babe was unusual. Mark Wilton's
baby was doing the part in 'The Lost Child' and
the babe was supposed to have been taken into an
inn and was to make its reappearance on a tray.
After the babe's first exit it got to crying so terribly that it could not reappear and I recall how
Mr. Maiben was dancing a jig all over the stage

saying, 'What shall we do, what is to be done?' In the terrible anxiety I grabbed Maude from the cradle, put her on the tray and she was taken on. Of course the child had grown immensely from a few minutes previous and Maude amused the whole audience by sitting up and cooing to them."

When her mother died Maude came from New York to arrange for the funeral. The automobile was just beginning to replace the horse-drawn carriage, but Maude insisted that the cortege be made up entirely of carriages drawn by white horses. It was necessary to search the entire valley before enough of them could be found, but the required number was finally secured, and a picturesque procession they made indeed as they moved slowly on to the cemetery.

Father made it a special point to see that the women who were acting at the theatre were not allowed to be out alone at night, especially if they had any great distance to go to the theatre from their homes. In such instances he always sent his carriage to take them back and forth. If the company went out to play in some other town, as occasionally happened, they were most carefully chaperoned. At one time when they were playing in Ogden a young man became interested in one of the girls and wanted an introduction. In order to further his purposes, he took Mr. Harris, the announcer, out to dinner. When he pleaded his cause, however, Mr. Harris refused, gently but firmly, saying, "I can't. It would be worth my job."

Father had not, at first, shown any great cordiality to the idea of allowing Sara Alexander to become a member of the theatrical company, but her splendid work there won his complete approbation in time. An Eastern actor, who played in the city for a season, fell in love with her, and as she had no other guardian, came and asked for Father's consent to their marriage. Father replied, "Young man, I have seen you attempt Richard III, and Julius Caesar with fair success, but I advise you not to aspire to Alexander."

There was a private entrance to the theatre for our family, and as the doorman knew all of us it was never necessary for us to have tickets. We had our own special seats in the theatre as well. The girls of the family sat in the first row behind the parquet in what was known as the "dress circle." The first few front rows on the east side were reserved for the boys, and the wives sat in the west front section.

There was one drawback to going in through the family entrance. We missed the little old lady who stood on the front steps, very much bundled up against the cold, and sold apples and candy animals. We learned to value our good fortune, however, in being allowed to go as often as we pleased when we saw some of our friends carrying drinking water in the third circle in order to earn their tickets. One of these lads was Heber J.

Grant. He was graduated from water boy to actor for one performance when, at the age of thirteen, he played one of the pickaninnies in "Uncle Tom's Cabin."

Up in the first circle on the west side was the section reserved for the demimondes of the city, and they were never allowed to sit anywhere else. We children were not supposed to pay any attention to them whatsoever, but they were so pretty with their rouge, which no one else wore in that day, that I never could resist looking at them when I had a good opportunity.

Father had the upper box on the east side, and very often I would go with him and enjoy the performance by his side. Between acts he would take me by the hand and go out on a little balcony that led from the hall back of the box and stand there unobserved but observing. Sometimes we would go downstairs or backstage to see that all was well. Only once I remember of going down under the theatre with Father. The place was one of great mystery and seemed like another world.

He had a wonderful pair of opera glasses, which I had used many times and to which I had become very much attached. The glasses had three lenses, theatre, field, and marine. They were encased in leather and bore his initials on the outside. After his death, all his personal belongings were placed on auction for the members of the family since the executors felt that it would be impossible to distribute them fairly among so many of us. I had used these glasses so much that I was determined to have them, but, as another sister had the same idea, the bidding went so high that I was finally forced to pay $95 in order to obtain them. Years later when the leather had become somewhat worn I sent them to Tiffany's for repairs, in care of Spencer Clawson. Mr. Tiffany was very much intrigued with the glasses, said that he had never seen a pair quite like them, and offered to pay almost any amount of money for them. Naturally they were invaluable to me and are still in my possession.

Throughout the years in which I attended performances at the theatre my admiration went from one leading man to another until by the time I was grown the object of my devotion was Maurice Barrymore, the father of John and Lionel. About this time I took my first trip East, and while in the city of New York I searched the shops up and down Broadway for his photograph. There seemed to be any number of pictures of other actors, but the only one I could find of Barrymore showed him embracing his wife, Georgie Drew, while she looked up at him adoringly, which was not at all the type I had been searching for. However, since it was the only one I could find, I bought it and vented my wrath upon Georgie Drew by blacking both of her eyes. Later, in a more gentle mood, I attempted to erase the blacking but found that it had been done much too effectively.

From the day the theatre opened until the close

of his life in 1877, a period of fifteen years, Father maintained a deep interest in the affairs of the theatre. He frequently inspected the building and often attended rehearsals personally. Sara Alexander said of him: "Brigham Young knew more about the needs of a large stage than any manager now living." Even in later years when it was impossible for him to attend the performances regularly, he was kept informed of its affairs and, to a great extent, directed its policy.

He insisted that all entertainments be conducted with the strictest regard to moral conduct. None of the actors were allowed to smoke. The rehearsals of the home dramatic companies were opened with prayer, and there were instances where improper conduct on the part of the performers caused their instant dismissal.

He always preferred the lighter type of entertainment and once said, "If I had my way, I would never have a tragedy played on these boards. There is enough tragedy in every day life and we ought to have amusement when we come here." At one time when "Oliver Twist" was being played, a visiting star gave vent to a bit of realism where she was supposed to be killed by Bill Sykes in such a manner that Father declined to allow the play to be repeated.

Above all was he solicitous for the safety of the audience. Alfred Lambourne in his book, *A Playhouse*, comments on his careful supervision of the building: "It was upon the Scene-Painter's Gallery that the writer first met Brigham Young. It was a late afternoon in autumn; the rehearsal for that night's play was over, the Scene-Painter's brush was moving rapidly upon the broad spread of canvas before him and he thought himself alone. Anon was heard the sound of firm, yet almost inaudible footsteps upon the gallery stars. Then the maker appeared, and it was the President, the great Mormon leader. Unheralded he had come upon a tour of inspection. Brigham Young was famed for completeness; he possessed a genius for details. Carefully the President examined each watertank, each barrel of salt. He appeared to think that day of the Playhouse's danger from fire. He broke with the end of his gold-headed cane the thick crusts that had formed over the tops in the barrels of salt. I watched him shake his head and compress his lips; there came a frown upon his face. His orders for safety, one could see, had been neglected. He did a labor which should have been remembered and performed by others. No doubt someone would be reprimanded."

It was not strange that Father should have made this great effort to construct a theatre, for he never felt that his responsibilities to his people ended with his spiritual leadership. As one writer said of him: "A more remarkable combination of the esthetic, spiritual and practical, was seldom found in any man than marked the character of Brigham Young."

SOCIAL AFFAIRS

One of Father's most outstanding qualities as a leader was the manner in which he looked after the temporal and social welfare of his people along with guiding them in their spiritual needs. On the great trek across the plains when everyone but the most feeble walked the greater part of the way, the Saints would be gathered around the campfire for evening entertainment, if the weather was at all favorable. There songs would be sung, music played by the fiddlers, and the men and women would forget the weariness of walking fifteen miles or so over a trackless desert while they joined in dancing the quadrille. It was his way of keeping up "morale" before such a word was ever coined.

During the first few years after the arrival of the pioneers in the valley the dirt floors of the log cabins sufficed for the dances and socials that were a regular and important part of their lives. There was little furniture in the best of the homes, but what there was couldn't be damaged by being set outdoors, so the rooms were cleared, and through many a winter night could be heard the strains of the violins accompanying the dancers.

One of the first socials of which there is any record took place on Christmas night in 1850. A pioneer mother wrote of the affair: "On this day I went to Brigham's mill to a Christmas party. Stayed all night. We had a first rate supper at midnight. I helped to get it on the table. They danced all night until 5 o'clock in the morning the party broke up."

That same year an amusement house was built at the warm springs to be used almost exclusively for dancing. Being elevated from dirt to wooden floors, the parties promptly took on a much more cosmopolitan air, some of them even becoming "balls." For instance, there was the "Grand Military Ball" given by Professor Ballo's band for which the price of admission for a lady and a gentleman was three dollars. There was so little money in the valley that I cannot imagine how he even found enough people to make his ball successful at three dollars a couple. In all probability it was three dollars' worth of whatever produce the ticket purchaser happened to have in the granary.

The warm springs amusement hall was so far away from the center of the city (something over one mile) that a new building known as the Social Hall was erected in 1852 on State Street just one-half block south of the Eagle Gate. It was small but well built and, to our way of thinking, very fine indeed. At the west end was the door and at the east end a comparatively large stage. On ordinary occasions, when no play was being produced, the stage held a big stove, sofa, and easy chairs. On one side of the stove was a little table with a pitcher of water and tumblers, and when the scenery was on the stage, the big, black stovepipe still rose above in all its grandeur. There were no curtains at the windows, but they were decorated with red velvet lambrequins, and the benches, which ran all the way around the room from door to stage, were decorated in matching velvet. Two chandeliers provided a final note of elegance. It was here that all important functions took place for many years.

Not for their work alone were the pioneers called "hardy," for they attacked their amusements in the same gallant stride. Ballo's military ball commenced at 4 P.M. and lasted until long after midnight. A printed announcement for a party that Father gave in Social Hall in 1853 gives the opening hour as 2 P.M. precisely and states that supper would be served at 6 P.M. At midnight they usually had more refreshments before going on with the dance.

Long before I was old enough to attend the parties at Social Hall, I listened in envy to my older sisters as they described those wonderful balls. Especially was I intrigued with the details of the military ball given by the battalion of life guards when the hall was decorated with circles of sabers artistically arranged around the room while rifles glistened in every window. At one end of the hall was the flag of the minutemen with its motto "Always Ready," and at the other end the flag of the Stars and Stripes covered the entire breadth of the room. I was quite sure that such elegance never had been before nor would be again.

Another affair which I heard much about, but in more or less whispered tones around the house, was the ball given in honor of General Connor before his departure from Camp Douglas for a season in the spring of 1865. It seemed that some of the officers' ladies, preferring not to mingle with the Mormon women, declined to attend and that some of the Mormon ladies, feeling equally exclusive, also stayed away. Those who had risen above their prejudice, however, and attended the ball had described it as being most delightful.

To my great happiness, the day finally arrived when I, too, was permitted to attend the parties at Social Hall. I did not go to participate in the dancing, of course, as I was still only a child, but merely to sit on the side lines and watch the older people dance. Father was an excellent dancer and could turn a "pidgeon wing" with the best of them. I remember, too, that he was always plentifully supplied with partners. During the intermission he would often bring a number of guests home to the Beehive House for supper, and this brought an end to my part in the festivities for I was sent to bed instead of being allowed to go back again. On one occasion when we arrived at the house Mother said to me, "Is the party out already?"

And I answered—as I thought, very brightly—
"Oh, no. It's just retribution."

Occasionally suppers were served in the basement of the Social Hall, sometimes very elaborate
affairs costing as much as five dollars a couple. I
remember one very fine supper that Mr. Golightly,
the baker, had prepared. I went downstairs holding fast to Father's hand and stood close beside
him in one of the narrow aisles between the tables
while he talked for a few minutes with his counselor George A. Smith. Brother Smith was a very
large man, probably weighing about 350 pounds
and, not seeing me at all, he stepped on my foot.
I thought I had been very nearly killed.

While Father enjoyed having his friends come
to our home for suppers he was not at all inclined
to going other places to eat. Whether it was because he was partial to Mother's cooking or wasn't
quite sure of the cleanliness in other people's
homes, I do not know. I am inclined to think that
the latter reason may have entered in somewhat,
for I remember hearing him say upon one occasion when I was accompanying him and Mother
out to dinner, "Now, Lucy, I want you to be sure
and see that Jane doesn't make our tea out of the
same water that she boils the eggs in."

Almost from the very first, Social Hall was too
small for the crowds who came to attend the
parties, and before long it became necessary to
issue tickets of different colors for certain dances

(Photo Courtesy L.D.S. Church Information Service)   Sitting Room — Beehive House

so that everyone would have a chance to participate.

Very popular, indeed, were the leap-year parties of which the ladies took every advantage. One such ball caused quite a furore among some of the prominent women in charge of the affair because a lively young girl had the temerity to ask Father to attend the dance with her after the committee had practically worked themselves greyheaded in selecting a suitable partner for him.

The girl was Belle Park, a daughter of Father's overseer, Hamilton Park, and as her mother was a member of the committee and the committee meetings were held at her home, she had ample opportunity to overhear the plans. After a great deal of discussion they had finally decided that the actress Nellie Colebrook would be the logical person for the honor of escorting Father to the ball and that the committee would go to her in a body and apprise her of their decision.

Belle quickly made a decision of her own, however, and running the short distance between the two homes, arrived breathless at our door. Mother answered her knock and said, "What can I do for you, Belle? You look as if you had something important on your mind."

"I have," she answered. "I must see President Young immediately."

Mother took her into Father's office, and after he had greeted her, she said briefly, "I have come to invite you to the leap-year ball."

Father glanced at Mother with a twinkle in his eye and said, "Well, Lucy, I've heard a lot about this ball and concluded that I was going to be a wall flower. Bring your carriage to the door, young lady, and I shall be ready."

As the Parks had no carriage, Father took his and called for Belle and her parents also. The committee were quite indignant when they learned that a seventeen-year-old girl had thwarted their plans, but as there was nothing they could do about the matter it was allowed to drop.

Besides the balls at Social Hall, dances were frequently held in the ward meetinghouses. For a long time the tickets were paid for in produce, the party-goer coming with a basket on one arm containing the price of his admission and one on the other arm containing the picnic for his evening's refreshment. And, of course, there was the ever popular home party with the entertainment consisting of pulling molasses candy, husking corn, or else spelling or apple bees.

The larger socials were held in the great theatre after it was completed in 1862. A temporary floor could be laid even with the stage over the seats on the lower floor, and the playhouse with its elegant appointments, made a very beautiful ballroom indeed for these people not yet two decades in this desert country.

In our own family life recreation always played an important part, for Father believed firmly that everyone should have a proper amount of work, rest, and play during each day. Many were the outings and picnics which we enjoyed, sometimes with others of the community and sometimes with only the members of our own family. Two favorite places for our family excursions were the Brighton Resort in Big Cottonwood Canyon, and the Great Salt Lake. It seems strange now that we would have taken the trouble to go to either in the cumbersome wagons of the day.

In 1856, just nine years after the valley was first settled, Father sent out formal printed invitations to a "Pic-nic Party" at the headwaters of Big Cottonwood "Kanyon." A footnote informed the invited guest that he would be required to start very early as no one would be permitted to pass the first mill, about four miles up the "Kanyon," after 2 P.M. I presume this was to make sure that no one was on the road after dark. With wagons, it required two days' travel to reach the camping ground. Once there, however, the entrancing beauty of the place, the singing, and general merrymaking made all the laborious effort of reaching there seem worth while.

The beach of the Salt Lake is twenty miles away from the city, and while the road is not a steep, mountainous one like the other, still a very early start was necessary if we were to go there and back in a day. When we arrived at the lake we would go to the huge black rock for the protection of a dressing room since there is not a single tree within many miles of the salt-encrusted shore of the lake. There was an elevated pathway which led from the shore to the rock. Father would say, "The girls to the left and the boys to the right," and we girls would march around and put on the linsey dresses and pantalettes that we used for swimming, or rather floating, in the buoyant waters, while the boys donned their customary bathing suits of overalls and shirts. After the swim we would enjoy the sumptuous lunch that the clan from the Lion and Beehive Houses always brought along on any outing.

At various times attempts were made to use large pleasure boats on the lake but never with any great degree of success. Father built and launched the first boat of any consequence to sail the lake in the year 1854. The boat was forty-three feet long and designed for a stern wheel to be propelled by horses working a treadmill. It was to be used partly to transport stock between the city and Antelope Island as well as for pleasure trips on the lake. There was a formal christening party when the boat was named the *Timely Gull* in the presence of several of Father's friends and members of his family. The *Timely Gull* was not destined to sail the salty waters of the lake for very long, however, being wrecked by a gale and strewn along the shore after making only a few trips.

The next boat of importance on the lake was the *City of Corinne*, which was purchased by the Church in Chicago, dismantled, and shipped here to be used largely for commercial purposes. The boat met the same fate as her predecessor and was wrecked by gales on the rocks in the vicinity of Mount Hogg.

Captain Garfield, a wealthy mining man from California, made the next boating venture on the Great Salt Lake with a steamboat which he christened the *Garfield*. This large pleasure boat was for many years the pride of the lake, but when it, too, was blown from its moorings and wrecked, it was salvaged and converted into a bathing resort with kitchen, dining room, and dressing rooms.

It was during our earliest courting days that the *Garfield* was at the height of its popularity, and naturally I was very much thrilled when John asked if he might take me out there to spend the evening. As he was making only three dollars a week, Mother put up a lunch for us, filling a fair-sized chip basket with delicious sandwiches and cakes. When John arrived at our home, however, he would have none of the lunch basket, declaring with pride that he intended to take me to the restaurant for supper. I wouldn't hurt Mother's feelings for the world after she had gone to so much trouble, so I said with determination, "We're not going without this lunch."

With equal determination John said, "Well, we're not going with the lunch." And we were both right. We stayed home.

Father always loved to take visitors to the city out for a swim in the lake, and often I was included in the party. At first we used to go in a spring wagon or the victorine, but after the narrow-gauge railroad was built he had a private car for such occasions. At one time when he was taking a party out, some notable man asked me what percentage of salt the lake waters held. Not having the faintest idea, but feeling that I must answer anyway, I promptly replied, "Ninety-five per cent." "My dear child," he said with a kindly but "how can you be so dumb?" look, "if it were that much, the lake would be solid salt."

On rare occasions we crossed the waters of the lake over to Antelope Island. At one time Father had planned to establish a Church farm there for the raising of cattle and horses. A five-room house was built near the largest spring, and for some years it was used for outings by various of the Church officials. There was some evidence that Kit Carson had once used it as a rendezvous, and a canoe, which was supposedly left there by him, has a place in the Church museum along with his rifle.

Much as we enjoyed these outings to the lake or the near-by canyons, a dance always held first place in our interest. The girls were allowed to go quite freely to the dances in the ward halls, but they loved also to go occasionally to the courthouse, and it was there that Father began to shut down on them. The courthouse really was only the upper floor of a large building on Main Street which was sometimes the scene of social affairs because of its size.

On one occasion a party had been announced and invitations sent out with the names of all the members of the committee printed thereon as was the custom. Nearly all of our girls had accepted invitations to the dance, myself included, and consternation was widespread among us when Father said that we were not to attend the party. Father usually meant no when he said it, and the girls were just heartsick over the whole affair, having hopefully given their promises to their best beaux and pressed up their best gowns in anticipation of the event.

As a last resort my older sister Mira came to me and said, "Clint, we've just got to go to this party. You can always get around Father. You see what you can do about it." I was awfully anxious to go myself as I was just now beginning to go to parties, and the handsome young John Spencer had invited me to go with him, so I said, "I'll see what I can do."

I waited until after breakfast the next morning before I approached Father, for I knew that he would be in a good humor then. The building was owned by a man named Groesbeck, and here I believe I showed some of Father's own diplomacy for instead of mentioning the courthouse I said, "There's going to be a party in *Brother Groesbeck's* building, and we girls would like very much to go."

Father sat for a while and twirled his thumbs around each other as he always did when he was thinking, and finally he said, "Who's on the committee? Are there any Gentiles?" When I assured him that the committee was above reproach he continued, "Well, you children have always been taught to behave yourselves. If you will go and not mingle with the Gentiles, I guess you can go." I gave him a grateful kiss and ran off to tell the good news to my waiting sisters.

While we girls were usually very careful to obey our parents and associate only with members of our own faith, there occasionally were times when we did "mingle with the Gentiles." I remember in particular one nice-looking boy who had come from the East and was staying with relatives while he studied chemistry at the Deseret University. He had a fine horse and buggy, always a superior attraction for a girl of my day, and I loved to go riding with him. I figured that it was all right for me to go for he was a perfect gentleman and I knew how to behave. I also figured that there was no need to distress my parents about the matter, so I was always very careful to get out of the buggy a block or so from home, being a firm believer in the convenient axiom that what they didn't know wouldn't hurt them.

All was not playtime for the boys and girls in the Lion and Beehive Houses, however. Although there were about twenty-five hired men and women on the place, each one of us was expected to do some share of the work. During the fruit season or housecleaning time, especially, we joined forces with our mothers and the maids and expended our best energies on the peaches or the dust as the case might be.

On Sunday there was neither any work nor play in our home that could possibly be avoided. Father observed the Sabbath with a Puritanical strictness and insisted that everyone else do the same. Not only the members of the family but the hired help as well were expected to make it a day of rest. The big dinner of the week was served on Saturday so that there would be cold meat left over for the Sunday dinner. The horses were never used if it were at all possible to avoid doing so, and even the machinery on the place was given a day of rest. Father would never wear the same clothes on Sunday that he wore on other days and he always urged his family to follow the same rule.

If we indulged in singing or reading, the music or books must be of a nature appropriate to the day. Of course, we were always expected to be in church during every session that was held so that we often attended twice or even three times a day. The girls' beaux could come on Sunday nights and be entertained in the parlor, but if the young people went buggy riding they must do so on some other night of the week.

When I grew old enough to be going out on Sunday night the young people of my age would entertain in groups. We would all attend church first, and then after meeting we would take a nice long walk in the dusk of the evening, ending up at the home of one of the crowd where we would have milk and doughnuts or occasionally some good homemade ice cream. No movies, jazz, or automobile rides—how tame it would all seem to the youth of today. But we enjoyed it, and I shall always be grateful for the wholesome atmosphere that surrounded my early girlhood.

The Beehive House was built with the purpose in view of having a place large enough for the entertainment of Father's visitors and friends and held spacious parlors both upstairs and down that were well suited to its purpose for that day.

Of all the parties and receptions that took place in the Beehive House, quite naturally none stands out in my memory as does my own lovely wedding reception. Rather oddly, only two of Father's daughters had wedding receptions in the Lion or Beehive Houses, the other one being my half sister Nabbie, who married Spencer Clawson. The principal reason for this was that many of the girls married in polygamy, and so of course the weddings were very quiet affairs with perhaps only a special dinner by way of festivity. The ceremonies themselves always took place in the Endowment House, which was used for these ordinances before the Temple was finished.

My own two older sisters were both plural wives, and while they were very happily married, one of them to the husband of another half sister, they had no receptions to mark their weddings. When my turn came along, being the last of Mother's daughters and having my John all to myself, I decided to have a large reception.

Although my marriage took place some years after Father's death, I was very happy in the knowledge that he had known my chosen husband and approved of him. We had been sweethearts since we were little more than children, and I recall that I was only in my very early teens when Father first learned of my interest in John. John was ill at the time with typhoid fever, and quite often I would take some pigeons and a bucket of milk down to him. One day as I was walking through the office on my way out, Father stopped me and said, "Daughter, what have you got there?" I told him that Mother had fried some pigeons and was sending them with a quart of new milk to John Spencer, who was ill. "And who is John Spencer?" he asked. I replied rather proudly that he was the son of Daniel and Emily Spencer. Father gave me his slow smile, which was always so benign and warming, as he answered, "A fine boy, and fine parents. Take good care of him." And I have tried to do so ever since.

It was in order that I might have the small front parlor for entertaining John that Father moved over to the Lion House—just another incident of his constant thoughtfulness for the comfort and welfare of his family. The death of my youngest brother Feramorz had taken place very suddenly and tragically at sea, only a few months before John had asked me to marry him, and I felt that I couldn't leave Mother alone in her sorrow in this great house. When we told her our plans for our future happiness, however, she urged that the marriage take place soon and that we make our home with her in the Beehive House. This suggestion made us very happy, of course, and we immediately began preparations for our wedding and decided that it should take place within a few months.

My wedding dress was not made in the style of the eighties but was fashioned after a dress I had seen a Mrs. Leslie, an actress, wear when I was a very little girl. Mrs. Leslie had come to Salt Lake with the Irwins in the early sixties, and accompanying her was a young niece, Flora Bray. The latter gave me an adorable miniature gold album which I was greatly tempted to give to Colleen Moore for her doll house when she exhibited it here recently and probably would have done so had not my daughters demurred. I admired these people very much and decided even at that early day that when the time came for me to wear a wedding gown it should be made like the princess style dress worn by Mrs. Leslie.

We made the dress at home, so I had it just as I wanted it. The material was of heavy white brocaded satin, and a piece was sent to Laird, Shoeber, and Mitchell in Philadelphia so that I might have slippers made to match my gown. My stockings were of heavy ribbed silk which today would look more like golf socks than wedding stockings, but at that time they were wonderful to me.

Preparations for the supper began days and days ahead of the wedding day. Mother cooked and cooked, and so did everyone in the house who could wield an egg beater or measure a cup of flour. We prepared hams, tongues, turkeys, and chickens. We sent to California for gallon cans of peaches, pears, and cherries. Talula and I made cakes for three days—white cakes, gold cakes, layer cakes, cream cakes, and sponge cakes. Mother made the doughnuts, mince pies, and salads, and dear Aunt Eliza Burgess Young made the wedding cake with its many tiers, which Brother Brown, the caterer, iced and decorated.

On the morning of the wedding, John called for me in a big barouche drawn by a fine span of horses. No one could possibly have come in finer style nor have looked more handsome. The dress I wore to the Endowment House was of navy blue with a velvet skirt and a satin basque trimmed with cut-steel buttons. My hat was a dark blue velvet elongated turban with an ostrich feather on the left side and a little bird ornament in front. My wrap was a long grey and black ulster that I had worn to New York two years before and, as usual, I wore high, black, laced shoes.

My sisters Fanny and Talula comprised all our wedding party. When we reached the Endowment House where we were to be married, we were so early that we had to sit down on a bench outside and wait for the building to be opened—not a very dignified procedure for a bride and groom who had proved to be a trifle too impatient. I was far too happy, however, to let a little thing like waiting outside a church bother me.

After our marriage we went home to a quiet luncheon with members of my own family. Just before we sat down Mother called one of the maids to get some fresh water for lunch, but John, in his gallant way, insisted that he be allowed to get it. In a few minutes he came marching back in again, proudly bearing the coal scuttle which he had picked up in the kitchen and filled with water at the pump in the back yard without ever noticing his mistake. Of course everyone laughed, but I thought it an evidence of how much in love he was.

The house had been literally turned upside down and inside out for the wedding. Beds had been taken down, long tables set in the big front room downstairs where supper was to be served to 350 guests, and fires had been laid in the two Franklin stoves in the upstairs parlor, where we were to receive.

The wedding reception was as beautiful in every detail as I had hoped for in my fondest dreams. After the guests had come and gone with their many expressions for our happiness, the lights were all turned out, the fires seen to for safety, the doors locked, Mother's good-night kiss and

Lion and Beehive Houses

embrace given, John and I went to our room. It was very late, and all had seemed quiet for a long time when a timid knock came on our door. I called out, "Mother, is that you? Come in." Mother opened the door and, holding her candle high above her head, walked up to the bed and said, "Clarie, *do* you know where I put the key to the little bedroom downstairs? I have been looking for nearly two hours for it and cannot find it."

The missing key belonged to the little room where Mother and I had slept the night before and which held the only available bed in the house, for the hired help filled all the others. I said that I couldn't remember seeing it anywhere but would get up and help look for it. Suddenly I said, "Mother, have you looked in the pocket of your petticoat?" She put down the candle, raised her skirt, and put her hand in her pocket and drew out the key. Then looking at us with a weary smile, she said, "Sure enough, here it is. Well, good night, children." Poor, dear Mother! Wandering around the house for two hours after all the labors of that day.

In 1932 we went back to the Beehive House for a reception in honor of our golden wedding anniversary. I held my bouquet in the same little holder of lace paper and tinfoil that John had given me on our wedding day. Many of our original presents were on display, and many of the same guests were invited. At my side stood a slender young niece in my white satin wedding gown.

HOLIDAYS

Father loved children very much and made our home entertainments and holidays just as delightful as the facilities of the day would permit. The Christmas celebrations of my childhood hold memories that are especially dear to me. No one in the entire household was ever forgotten, and this meant providing Christmas cheer for a great many people when one included the help and pensioners on the estate as well as the family.

Simple as our celebrations were, our elders were fond of reminding us how very much more fortunate we were than the children of two decades earlier when a good square meal was ample cause for celebrating any day in the year. The first Christmas in the valley—so we were told—everyone worked as usual. The men gathered sagebrush and some of them even plowed, for there was little snow and the ground was still soft. Christmas came on Saturday, but Saturday being a workday not even Christmas could interfere with the usual labors, and so the celebration was held on the Sabbath. Nearly everyone was still living in the old fort, and they all gathered around the flagpole in the center of the square, sang, prayed, shook hands, and joined around a sagebrush fire. They were completely filled with joy that their lives had been preserved in the great trek and that they had found a home where they might enjoy peace. They asked for nothing more.

By the time another Christmas rolled around many had moved from the fort to homes of their own, and there was considerably more of feasting and good cheer. One of the pioneers, Mrs. Catherine Wooley, wrote in her journal: "S.A. took the things out of the house. Betsy mopped the floor and I did the cooking. Had seventeen couples to eat besides E.D. and children, Betsy, Samuel and I. Got dinner over and then went in the house and took a rest; had refreshments at eight o'clock and at one and at three. The company was very quiet and did well; had a fine dance. December 26 clear and cold. The company left this morning after sunrise. We cleaned up and sent the borrowed dishes home. Pie and cake to the Dr. All well this evening only I am very tired."

Within the short space of three years the population of the city had increased to thousands, and the Christmas celebration took on a still greater air of gaiety. A brass band paraded up and down the streets, with the players mounted on horseback. They serenaded at Father's house as well as the homes of other Church leaders. All the toys were home made, the ads in the paper carrying no mention of commercial playthings. However, if a husband wished to delight his wife with a new bonnet on Christmas morning, there was Mrs. A. Smith, "Late of St. Louis," who advertised a su-

perior assortment of velvet, silk, satin, and straw
bonnets, and a variety of fancy goods and
millinery.

For days before Christmas I would slip into the
family store, north of the Beehive House, and
watch John Haslam tie up little square packages
of nuts and raisins during his spare time. It was
doubly worth my while because I could always
count on his slipping me a lump of sugar or some
other tasty bit while he was working. We would
receive these nuts and raisins on Christmas morning along with vinegar and molasses candy that
the girls had made and an abundance of "store"
candy—gumdrops and peppermint sticks.

There was no tree in our home, for at that time
the Christmas tree had not even come into general
use in the East, but we always hung up our stockings, and every child received one toy and some
clothing. We girls would receive knitted scarves,
nubias (headdresses), mittens, shoes, stockings,
garters, and wristers. John Spencer's first present to me was a pair of silk knitted wristers for
which he had spent an entire week's wages. I
nearly died of humiliation when a young nephew
said scornfully right in his presence, "Is *that* all
you brought her?" Some of us younger girls once
received some red cashmere hoods that Mother's
sister had made for us. They were made with a
pointed cape in the back and trimmed with white
swansdown and would have been rather pretty
except that they had been lined with green cambric

and tied with green ribbons because they were the
only materials available in the house. As it was,
they were a dreadful mixture of colors, and I
hated them vehemently.

The boys would often receive new capes for
Christmas, those being the outer garment most
commonly worn. My brother Ernest, who was a
big, husky fellow and didn't feel the cold very
much, would wear his about his waist in skirt
fashion to the great amusement of the rest of us.

For Christmas toys the boys would get swords,
drums, guns, and skates while we girls would be
made happy with wooden-headed dollies. The
heads were turned in our own carpenter shop, then
painted and sewed onto cloth bodies. When the
dolls were finished they would be beautifully
dressed by our diligent mothers. There was a
Betsy Long who had a shop on Main Street where
she made lovely wooden dolls, and conveniently
near by was a woman basketmaker who could
make equally fine bassinets.

My first wax doll, Lucy Ann, was among the
first shipment of dolls to come to Utah, and she
has now become quite a historic lady. She was
not given to me for Christmas but on a decidedly
different occasion. Father had been in the habit
of pulling my baby teeth as they came loose. His
ingenious procedure was to go to the cupboard in
his room and get a nice long string of rock candy
to dangle before my eyes. He would tell me to
eat it, and if the tooth did not come out with the

candy he would examine it. I see now the wonderful psychology he used even in his dealings with children. If the tooth did not come out with the candy and he had to come to the rescue, I would never see the forceps.

When the time came for the extraction of my first double tooth he urged me to go to Dr. Sharp, the family dentist—I am quite sure because he was loathe to hurt me himself. I did not want to go, and Father coaxed without avail. I don't seem to have been very susceptible to coaxing, but once more I succumbed to a bribe. Taking me on his knee, Father said, "Daughter, the Zion's Co-op has just received a shipment of wax dolls, such as you have never seen before. They are very beautiful and have real hair and shoes and stockings. If you will let Dr. Sharp pull your tooth I will have John Haslam go down with you the minute your tooth is out, and you can choose any doll you want for your own."

Such diplomacy won, of course. The doll is still very dear to me, with her features blurred from too frequent washings of oil, the only cleansing agent my mother said could be used safely. The hair is a trifle thin from constant combing during her early years, the grey plaster shoes show signs of wear, and the stockings are only half there, but precious she is, with the quite elaborate wardrobe I made for her in later years. My daughters and granddaughters have all enjoyed her, and soon a small great-granddaughter will be old enough to realize that Lucy Ann is something more than just another doll.

The first Thanksgiving Day in the valley was not celebrated in November but on New Year's Day instead. Apparently, Father thought the latter date more convenient or desirable at that particular time, and late in December of 1851 he issued the following unique proclamation:

"Proclamation of Gov. B.Y. issued in Dec. 1851.

"I, Brigham Young, Governor of the Territory aforesaid, in response to the time honored custom of our fathers at Plymouth rock, by the governors of the several states and territories, and with a heart filled with humility and gratitude to the Fountain of all good for his multiplied munificence to His children have felt desirous to and do proclaim Thursday, the first day of January eighteen hundred and fifty-two, a Day of Praise and Thanksgiving, for all the citizens of our peaceful territory. And I recommend to all the good citizens of Utah that they abstain from everything that is calculated to mar or grieve the spirit of their Heavenly Father, on that day; that they rise early in the morning of the first day of the New Year and wash their bodies with pure water; that all men attend to their flocks and herds with carefulness; and see that no creature in their charge be hungry, thirsty or cold, while the women are preparing the best of food for their households, and their children ready to receive it in cleanliness and with cheerfulness. I also do request of all good and peaceful citizens that they abstain from all evil thinking, speaking, and acting on that day; that no one be offended by his neighbor; that all jars and discords cease . . . that all may learn truth and have no need of priests to teach them. That all may do as they would be done by. I further request that when the day has been spent in doing good, in dealing out your bread, your butter, your port, your beef, your turkies, your molasses and the choicest of all products of the valleys of the mountains, at your command as to the poor; that you end the day in eating with singleness of heart as unto the Lord with praise and thanksgiving, and songs of rejoicing. Retire to your beds early and rise early again and continue doing good."

Thanksgiving was never a day of excessive feasting at our home. We would have a good dinner sufficient unto our needs, but prayer and thankfulness were the first order of the day.

On Father's birthday one of the wives, Aunt Margaret Pierce, would train the children of the family in songs and dances especially learned or made up in his honor. There was always a large dinner in the Lion House and greetings from the officials and members of the Church, but very seldom any presents. Almost the only present I remember the family giving him was a "hair wreath" now on display at the state capitol. Hair work was just coming in at that time, and several of the girls of the family took it up, but this particular wreath of flowers was a very grand one which was made professionally. Hair from the heads of every member of the family was used in its making. I have a hair bracelet which was made about the same time, and the links of gold which hold it together are made from some of the first gold found in California in 1849.

One present that Father received—not from the family, however—was a handsome barouche. It bore his coat of arms and made an elegant equipage for taking distinguished guests about the city, but Father didn't like it. He said that it was too fussy. The carriage intrigued me very much, however, and I was fond of riding about in it whenever I had an opportunity. It stood in a carriage house in the southeast corner of the grounds surrounding our home. A small stream of water for washing the carriage ran in and out of the carriage house by means of a small trough, and we children would sit by the hour on a hot summer day and dangle our feet into its pleasant coolness.

Another gift which Father received was a piece of beautiful black silk moire to be used in making a fancy vest. This he brought to me one day, saying that there was more than enough material in the piece for a vest and it was too fancy for him anyway, so that I might have it if I wished. I made myself an elegant coat out of the moire with passementerie trimming down the back—a coat which I still have.

July 24, the anniversary of the arrival of the first pioneers into the valley, has always been the occasion for special celebrations, but I doubt that one ever has or ever will equal the one held in 1849 on the second anniversary, considering the facilities of the times.

A large cannon had been brought from Nauvoo the first year, part of the way on its own wheels and the rest of the journey in a wagon, and on the day before the celebration several of the brethren spent the day making cartridges for firing salutes. Forty-niners, on their way to California, had obligingly furnished seventy-five pounds of powder toward the venture. At 7:30, on the morning of the twenty-fourth, when the great sixty-five-foot national flag was unfurled, it was saluted by the firing of this cannon, the firing of guns, the ringing of the Nauvoo bell, and spirit-stirring airs from the band.

The main events of the day were held in the Bowery, an open-air building on the Temple grounds, and hither at 3:15, Father and his counselors were escorted by the following retinue: (1) Horace S. Eldredge, marshal, on horseback, in military uniform; (2) brass band; (3) twelve Bishops bearing the banners of their wards; (4) seventy-four young men dressed in white, with white scarves on their right shoulders and coronets on their heads, each carrying in his right hand a copy of the Declaration of Independence and the Constitution of the United States, and each carrying a sheathed sword in his left hand. One of them carried a beautiful banner which bore the inscription, "The Zion of the Lord"; (5) twenty-four young ladies dressed in white with white scarves on their shoulders and wreaths of white roses on their heads, each carrying a copy of the Bible and Book of Mormon and one carrying a very neat banner inscribed with, "Hail to our Captain"; (6) Brigham Young, Heber C. Kimball, Willard Richards, Parley P. Pratt, Charles C.

Rich, John Taylor, Daniel Spencer, D. Fullmer, Willard Snow, and Erastus Snow; (7) twelve Bishops carrying flags of their wards; (8) twenty-four Silver Greys led by Isaac Morley, Patriarch, each having a staff painted red at the upper part and a bunch of white ribbon fastened at the top, one of them carrying the Stars and Stripes bearing the inscription, "Liberty and Truth."

As they left our house and marched through the streets the young men and women sang a hymn, the Nauvoo bell pealed, and the band played. When all had arrived at the Bowery, the audience, which had been waiting for an hour, shouted, "Hosanna to God and the Lamb!" and "Hail to the Governor of Deseret!" A meeting followed in which songs were sung and the Constitution of the United States was read and received with cheers.

The climax of the day came after the meeting, however. Canopies had been extended one hundred feet from each side of the Bowery, and beneath this awning dinner was served to several thousand people including some hundreds of California emigrants and threescore Indians.

The following year, the day was also celebrated in style, and I particularly love to think back on the description of the costume worn by the young ladies and young men in the parade which one observer chronicled: "The dress of 24 young ladies was white dress, blue sash and a pink and blue wreath of flowers on their heads. The gent's dress was white pants, red sash, blue coat and white hats with green ribbons and the choir was pink and white both gents and ladies."

Unique among all celebrations was that held on Independence Day in 1871 when the Mormons and the non-Mormons each held a separate celebration. The Mormons had a splendid procession, followed by a meeting in the Tabernacle where thousands of children sat in the center of the hall and sang. The actress Nellie Colebrook made a stately Columbia, with attendants representing the states and territories. In the audience sat the Hon. Elizabeth Cady Stanton and Susan B. Anthony.

The non-Mormons had a procession and a meeting likewise. In the first-named they featured the Goddess of Liberty in a float, carriages with state and army officials and several wagonloads of ore and bullion.

During the meetings each side threw dirt unsparingly at the other group, but, beyond that, the day passed off peaceably enough.

The celebrations within my own memory were wonderful, although exceedingly noisy ones, with a barrage of firecrackers and guns lasting through the entire night. At 5 A.M. the bands would play, and at sunrise a salute would be fired for each territory (rather than state, since Utah had not yet attained statehood). Of course the parades were always the high spot of the day, and it was surprising the ingenuity and sometimes the näiveté that was displayed in those pioneer processions.

There were sure to be a number of bands in any

parade, bands having always played an important part in life among our people. When the very first companies left Illinois on the trek across the country, although they didn't have sufficient food for their needs, they had *two* bands to help uphold their morale, one evidently not being deemed sufficient for the purpose. Father always had a float of the wonderful fruit that was grown upon our place, and many others drove wagons in which they proudly displayed the beautiful flowers and luscious fruits that they had brought forth from the desert. There was one parade in which twenty-four young girls, including myself, rode on horseback. We wore riding habits of white unbleached muslin, which I designed and helped make, and fetching little round caps patterned very much like those worn today.

We seldom had a "celebration" except on the regular holidays, but the coming of the first railroad train into Ogden was the occasion for one of the most spontaneous and rousing celebrations that I have ever seen. I was only nine years old at the time and had been taken to Ogden, along with my mother's young sister Christine, by Aunt Amelia. The forty-mile trip in the carriage meant a very early start if we were not to miss any of the excitement, but we enjoyed every minute of it, and Crissie and I spent much of the time wondering what a train would look like. I believe that even Aunt Amelia didn't know quite so much about a "modern" train as she pretended.

The entire affair more than surpassed our fondest expectations. The rails were being laid into the city by the workmen, and as soon as they were in place the train would move along behind. The "celebration" followed right along with the laying of the rails and the oncoming train. It is difficult now to imagine what the coming of the railroad meant to the people of that day. No more freighting of the most necessary supplies by ox team and wagon. No more weeks of weary, dusty travel in order to reach the civilization that lay beyond the mountains, and no more danger from Indians and robbers while attempting to cover the ground in a stagecoach. I think that my father must have been especially happy about it, because the bringing of thousands of converts to Utah, with the attendant hardships and dangers, had been one of his greatest problems during his leadership of the Church.

It was small wonder that the iron horse was greeted with near hysteria. People were all dressed up in their best, the city was gay with flags and bunting, and the lively music of bands filled the air.

The reviewing stand was located at a spot which the train reached by midafternoon. High above the stand waved the banner, "Hail to the Highway of the Nation. Utah Bids You Welcome," and on the stand sat high officials of the Church and Territory. As the train with its three engines steamed proudly up to the front of the stand, the din broke forth. There were three cheers for the highway, the artillery boomed, the bands played, and the engines whistled, while the excited people in the crowd shouted and waved their caps and hand-kerchiefs.

But all of this was quite insignificant in my mind beside the fact that I received a whole orange to eat by myself, the very first one I had ever had. To be sure, I had tasted one before. Father had come into the house one day after the arrival of an immigrant train and handed an orange to Mother, saying, "Lucy, here is an orange. Divide it among the children." He had shown her how to peel it, and it was divided into sections. I, being the youngest, also received the peelings, which I dried and treasured carefully for perfume.

This other, however, was quite different. Aunt Amelia, who was a very queenly woman and used to having about what she wanted, had seen the oranges and, turning to Hiram B. Clawson, had said, "Hiram, get me a bag of those oranges." Hiram complied, and Crissie and I each received one of them. So what mattered a train, even though we had never seen a train before and this one had three engines?

Just a few years previous to the coming of the "iron horse," the inauguration of Abraham Lincoln in 1865 had been the occasion for the greatest celebration in honor of a President that the city had ever seen. Lincoln had particularly endeared himself to the Mormons by saying, when asked what policy he intended to pursue regarding them, "I intend to let them alone." This was all the consideration that our people asked of any President and much more than they had received of some.

On the day of his second inauguration a procession one mile in length moved through the streets of the city. The day was a wintry one, and the participants rode in sleighs decorated with streamers and rosettes of red, white, and blue. As they passed by the houses, they were greeted with enthusiastic cheers from onlookers at the windows and even on the roofs. Later they assembled at a stand for a meeting, which was followed by a banquet given by the city council, which Colonel George and his staff of Camp Douglas attended as special guests. Fireworks in the evening completed the day's rejoicing.

Two months later the city was thrown into deep mourning over the sad news of the assassination. Flags were displayed at half mast, and many business houses and homes were draped in crepe. Father's carriage, covered with crepe, was driven through the city streets.

Certainly no occasion in Utah, during the nineteenth century, was more deserving of celebration than the day when the Territory was finally admitted into the Union.

The people had fought for statehood for a great many years but had been denied because of their attitude on the question of polygamy. Finally, on the fourth of January, 1896, the news was received by telegraph that the long-fought battle was won. The superintendent of the telegraph station attempted to announce it to the citizens by running out into the street and blowing off an old shotgun. For a time the frightened bystanders thought that a holdup was in progress and took shelter in the doorways of neighboring stores, but as the truth gradually became known and the good news spread, the city took on a festive appearance, with flags and bunting decorating every store window and home.

Needless to say, after waiting nearly fifty years for statehood, the people planned the finest celebration possible. The committee in charge of the meeting in the Tabernacle, at which the official announcement of statehood was to be made, decided that as one feature they would have a large flag made, large enough to cover almost the entire ceiling of that enormous building.

The appropriation for decorations was only seventy-five dollars, which was entirely inadequate, so two members of the committee, Spencer Clawson and Margaret Caine—determined that their undertaking should succeed—proceeded to call upon the merchants of the city for donations. By this means enough money finally was raised. George Romney, the manager of a local shoe factory, consented to make the flag for only twenty-nine dollars, the actual cost of the extra labor employed. The time of the regular employees and all of the thread used was given free of charge.

The flag, when finished, contained 1,296 yards of yard-wide bunting, each of the stripes being two yards in width. Its length was 132 feet and its width 78 feet. It was so heavy that it required the united efforts of eight men to lift and carry it into the building. Ropes were sewn into the edges, and after great exertion the flag was elevated to within nine feet of the ceiling, where it produced a most wonderful effect. The new "Utah" star was ingeniously lighted by cutting out the star shape from a square of black felt, covering the opening with plate glass and placing back of it, in a reflector, five thirty-two-candle-power electric lights. At that time it was the largest flag that had ever been made, and I doubt very much if it has been surpassed in size since.

During the meeting the military band played the "Star-Spangled Banner" just as the forty-fifth star shone forth in all its glory. Twelve hundred flags were used in decorating the Tabernacle, and the light bill alone was $120. A truly vast sum and a vast amount of light for those days. In the evening a magnificent ball was held in the theatre with such dances featured as the lancers, the quadrille, the two-step, and the Berlin polka.

Nearly all of the grown-up members of our family were in attendance, with the ladies outdoing all previous efforts in the matter of dress. Aunt Amelia wore a blue dress of lute-string silk trimmed with real Valenciennes lace, which was said to have cost several hundred dollars, and a number of my sisters wore creations almost as elegant.

VISITORS

The Beehive House was the only place suitable for the entertainment of notable visitors in whom Father was interested, the one or two hotels in the city making little pretense beyond keeping a guest reasonably comfortable. Our parlors were spacious and tastefully furnished, and Mother could always be depended upon to serve a meal to which he was proud to invite the most distinguished persons in the land. Many statesmen and Government officials were our guests during Father's lifetime for, even after he ceased being governor of the Territory, he was generally acknowledged to be in reality the head of the commonwealth which he had founded.

Among the prominent visitors from the East and from foreign countries that were entertained in our home were General Sherman and his daughter, James A. Garfield, Ole Bull (the Norwegian violinist), members of a Japanese embassy, Prince Frederick of Wittgenstein, who came with Baron Rothschild, and, greatest-sounding of all, the Emperor of Brazil. The latter may have been a very temporary ruler, I do not know, but he was most elegant, and I was greatly excited to have a personage of high title in our very own home.

One of the first of these famous guests was

(Photo Courtesy Deseret News)　　　A Parlor at the Beehive House

Horace Greeley, who came by stagecoach in 1859. Being a newspaperman, he was bold enough to question Father about the practice of polygamy, and Father discussed the matter very freely with him. Mr. Greeley next wanted to know whether Utah would be admitted as a free state or a slave state, to which Father replied: "She will be a free state. Slavery here would be useless and unprofitable. I regard it generally as a curse to the masters. I, myself, hire many laborers and pay them fair wages. I could not afford to own them. I can do better than subject myself to an obligation to feed and clothe their families and care for them in sickness and health. Utah is not adapted to slave labor."

Mr. Greeley stayed for more than a week before pressing farther on into that West which he became famed for endorsing as a suitable place for shaping the destinies of young men. During the course of his visit a large reception and banquet was given in his honor by the Deseret Typographical and Press Association.

The next year, also of necessity by stagecoach, came Richard F. Burton, an English officer famous for his explorations in Africa, and the inimitable Mark Twain. Burton had heard a great deal of unfavorable comment about the Mormons—there was practically no other kind in that day—and came all the way out here to see for himself. As a result of his visit he wrote a book, *The City of the Saints*, wherein he says of Father: "The first im-

pression left on my mind by this short visit, and
it was subsequently confirmed, was that the Prophet is no common man and that he has none of the
weakness and vanity which characterize the common man."

What Mark Twain thought of Salt Lake
City and of Father, we gather from his book,
Roughing It. What Father thought of Mark
Twain, I do not know, but I'm sure it wasn't what
the humorist would have us believe. Of the city
and its people he said: "We walked about the
streets of Great Salt Lake City and glanced in at
the shops and stores and there was a fascination
in staring at every creature we took to be a Mormon. We felt a curiosity to ask every child how
many mothers it had and if it could tell them
apart. . . . We strolled about everywhere through
the broad, straight, level streets and enjoyed the
pleasant strangeness of a city of 15,000 inhabitants with no loafers perceptible in it, and no visible drunkard or noisy people. A limpid stream
rippling and dancing through every street in place
of a filthy gutter; block after block of trim dwell-
ings built of frame and sunburned brick—a great
thriving orchard and garden behind every one of
them, apparently, and a grand general air of neat-
ness, repair, thrift and comfort around and about
and over the whole.

"Such was the home of the Latter Day Saints,
the stronghold of the prophets, the capitol city of

the only absolute monarchy in America, Great Salt Lake City."

Of his interview with Father he wrote: "The second day we put on white shirts and went and paid a state visit to the king (Brigham Young). He seemed a quiet, kindly, easy mannered, dignified, self-possessed old gentleman of fifty-five or sixty and had a gentle craft in his eye that probably belonged there. He was very simply dressed and was just taking off a straw hat as we entered. He talked about Utah and the Indians and Nevada and general American matters and questioned our secretary and certain government officials who came with us. But he never paid any attention to me, notwithstanding I made several attempts to 'draw him out' on Federal politics and his high-handed attitude toward congress. I thought some of the things I said were rather fine. But he merely looked around at me at distant intervals, something as I have seen a benignant old cat look around to see which kitten was meddling with her tail. By and by I subsided into an indignant silence and so sat until the end, hot and flushed and execrating him in my heart for an ignorant savage. But he was calm. His conversation with those gentlemen flowed on as sweetly and peacefully and musically as any summer brook. When the audience was ended and we were retiring from the presence, he put his hand on my head, beamed down at me in an admiring way and said to my brother, 'Ah—your child, I presume? Boy or girl?' "

One of the most unusual persons we ever entertained was the irrepressible George Francis Train, who although practically unknown to this generation attracted as much of the world's attention as any individual of his day not connected with official life. He was a man who gloried in taking the part of the underdog, and of course he found a most apt subject for his sympathies in the Mormons. He had spent part of the year 1869 in a British jail in Ireland, where he had landed for espousing the Fenian cause and upon being released, hastened to America to find new battles to fight.

During a tour of New England he gave an impromptu speech in defense of the Mormons which he had gleaned from one given in Congress by our representative William H. Hooper. The speech created a sensation, and from then on he took up cudgels for the cause and was constantly engaged in controversy with the press and his audiences.

He next came stumping across the country announcing his candidacy for the Presidency of the United States in 1872 and gave two addresses in Salt Lake City. He was a very large fellow with a mop of curly, bushy hair and many eccentricities of manner. His speeches made up in delivery what they lacked in content, and he was received with great enthusiasm.

The visit of Schuyler Colfax, Speaker of the

House, and his party in 1865 was, of course, a great occasion, since no one of such national importance had ever before braved the discomforts and dangers of a journey by stagecoach to gain firsthand knowledge of our Territory.

The party was met on a hill east of the city by an official welcoming party headed by the ex-delegate to Congress, William Hooper, who made a speech of welcome. Colfax responded in the fluent manner for which he was famous, and the party was then taken at once to the warm springs for a bath, which I have no doubt was most welcome. In the afternoon they attended a meeting in the Bowery, and on Saturday evening they were guests at a special performance in the theatre. One of the party in describing the performance said that "the playing, costumes and scenery were decidedly better than metropolitan theatres will average and the building in size and elegance was excelled by only five or six in the United States. The performance closed with an exquisite fairy spectacle which made it difficult to realize we were in the heart of the American desert."

Mr. Colfax did not think it becoming to his national importance to call upon Father (the only other person who had evinced such exclusiveness was the Indian chief, Walker), but when Father was so informed he went to call upon the Speaker, together with several of the Apostles. They had a very pleasant visit, which Mr. Colfax and his party later returned.

The Eastern visitors were the dinner guests of one of the leading merchants of the city, and one of them wrote of the affair: "A dinner to our party this evening at which President Young and the principal members of his council were present, had as rich a variety of fish, meats and vegetables, pastry and fruit as I ever saw on any private table in the east; and the quality and the cooking and the serving were unimpeachable. All the food, too, was native in Utah. The wives of our host waited on us most amicably and the entertainment was in every way the best illustration of the practical benefits of plurality that has yet been presented to us."

Of all the great men who called upon Father, I remembered best and admired most that fine gentleman and soldier, General William T. Sherman, Commander in Chief of the United States Army. He and his daughter were just returning from a tour of California and Oregon and made a brief stop in our city on their return East. They were staying at the Townsend House, and hundreds of people gathered in the street hoping that he would make a speech. At first he declined, but after a group of young choir girls had serenaded him with "Hard Times Come Again No More," he came out on the balcony and made a brief but earnest and sincere talk, telling them that he hoped that "hard times would come again no more" to our beautiful valley.

The next day he came to our home, and although

I was banished from the great presence while he paid his respects to Father, I gazed long and hard upon his retreating back, as he left, from the vantage point of an upstairs window.

Probably the guest who stayed with us for the longest period of time, and certainly under the most peculiar circumstances, was a Captain Evans. Father had been placed under arrest for resisting the United States authorities, but through the intervention of Colonel Kane, who was always his staunch friend, he was allowed to remain under arrest in his own home with a guard in the house. The guard, Captain Evans, lived at the Beehive House and ate his meals there, which, incidentally, raised the number of breakfasts that Mother had to prepare from three to four, for he always had his breakfast alone after the family had eaten. He was very courteous and agreeable, and some of my older sisters were quite taken with the handsome "Gentile." In fact, we were not at all sorry to have Father under arrest, especially since he came and went as he pleased anyway.

Father was very much interested in the theatre and often invited visiting stars, musicians, and other artists to our home. Among those I remember best were Julia Dean Hayne; Lingard, the monologist, and his wife "Dickie," who was very blonde and had a very sweet voice; the Swiss Bell Ringers, who made merry music upon bells set in frames and upon water glasses placed in rows on the table; the British Blondes, who put on the

light musical comedies that Father especially enjoyed; and Anna, the girl born without arms, who
wrote with her toes. She sat on the floor and handled, or rather "toed" the pen with as much fa-
cility as we who have the use of our hands can
do. I still have her letter to father in appreciation
of his hospitality.

But all of these fade into insignificance in com-
parison with the thrill I had when we received
Mr. and Mrs. Tom Thumb (Commodore Nutt and
Minnie Warren) as guests in our home. The other
children in the neighborhood could only see these
midgets on the stage, but I had the great pleasure
of sitting down to dinner at the very same table
with them. There is a story told that Tom Thumb,
looking up at Father, who was rather large in
build, said, "There is one thing that I can't understand and that is this belief in polygamy." Smiling
down at him, Father answered very genially, "I
couldn't understand it either when I was your
size."

Mrs. Hayne was by all odds the greatest favorite with our family as well as with the rest of the
community. Father admired her very much and
showed her every courtesy during her stay in the
city, which lasted an entire year. These courtesies
caused some gossip among the townspeople, and
there were rumors to the effect that she was secretly married to Father, all of them quite without
foundation. In a curtain call during her farewell
appearance she paid him a very lovely tribute, say-

ing, among other things, "To President Young, for many courtesies to a stranger alone and unprotected, I return these thanks which are hallowed by their earnestness, and I trust he will permit me, in the name of my art, to speak my high appreciation of the order and beauty that reigns throughout this house. I would that the same purity prevailed in every temple for the drama's teachings."

It was for her entertainment and in her honor that Father built and named our sleigh the "Julia Dean." The sleigh was a marvel in that day and would be a museum piece if it were still in existence. It was a great, long affair shaped something like a canoe, with the rear and front ends rising up very high and with the driver's seat placed between two graceful swans. It was drawn by six spirited horses and would seat twenty-four people comfortably, although when we children piled in for a merry ride over the frosty streets there was more likely to be twice that number tucked in between the buffalo robes and the blankets.

After the "Julia Dean" passed out of our possession it was used for a time as a band wagon and eventually wound up at a farm up in Davis County, where it served the lowly purpose of a feedbox for horses. Finally, one of the horses kicked it to pieces and brought an ignominious end to the once magnificent "Julia Dean."

It was in order to entertain his guests on a more elaborate scale that the Gardo House was built, although the popular rumor for many years was that it was built for Father's "favorite wife," Amelia Folsom, and it was commonly called "Amelia's Palace." The simple facts were that a more suitable place was needed, and Father was anxious to shift the burden of entertaining from Mother's shoulders.

Amelia may have been selected to act as hostess there, although she had no particular ability as a housekeeper, and it is true that she, together with Mary Ann Angell, was given a life lease upon the property at the time of Father's death, but the story of "Amelia's Palace" was the invention of a one-armed hack driver. He used to take tourists around the city to various points of interest and told this particular tale, along with many another colorful one, for the entertainment of his passengers. The house was not entirely finished when Father's death occurred, and both Aunt Amelia and Mother Young lived there only long enough to make their claims legal and then sold their leases to the Church.

After passing through the hands of two or three other people it became the property of Mrs. Emery Holmes, now the Princess Engalitcheff, who furnished it in regal style and gave elaborate entertainments there while she lived in Salt Lake. She insisted upon calling it "Amelia's Palace," and the name rather stuck until the house was torn down to make way for the Federal Reserve Bank. Father was very fond of giving names to all of his houses, and this particular one was named the

Gardo House from a Spanish book that he had particularly enjoyed.

He usually spent the winters down in southern Utah, where the climate is very mild, and although he made the original plans for the house, the partitions were partly put in place during his absence. The rooms were finished much too small for his liking, and he was quite disgusted with the place when he saw it. In fact, he remarked that he could never look at it without thinking of the Tabernacle organ.

A magnificent set of dishes and glassware decorated with the initials B.Y. in gold had been ordered for the house but arrived after Father's death. The executors of the estate decided to sell them to the interested members of the family and agreed that the amount raised on them should be five hundred dollars. The dishes were sold "unsight and unseen," for they still reposed in barrels in our large woodshed. When they were unpacked they were put into twenty-five piles, and numbers were drawn for them. I was among those who bought some of the dishes, and later my mother's and brother's share came to me so that I have rather a large amount of the "B.Y. China." Many of the grandchildren have expressed disappointment that none of it had come into their possession, but it was simply because their parents did not have the means or were indifferent about buying it at the time.

EARLY-DAY COMMUNICATION

The first mail carriers in Salt Lake City were the incoming settlers and the first post offices, the covered wagons which had traveled through deep rivers and rocky mountain passes for more than a thousand miles. The letters or newspapers might be anywhere from three to six months old, and the information they contained anything but "news." Letters informing friends or relatives of the impending arrival of emigrants would sometimes be delivered long after the senders themselves had made their appearance. The news that Utah had been created a Territory came through many months after the act had been passed by Congress.

But never were letters received more gratefully! For the first few years after the exodus began, the Saints were scattered all the way from Illinois to Salt Lake, and most of them were living in wagon boxes or temporary camps. Sickness and death were all too common among them, as those who had arrived in the valley first well knew. Late in the fall of 1848 Aunt Clara Decker wrote: "The excitement was great as Taylor and Green rode into the city and distributed the letters without envelopes, tied round and round with buckskin thongs." Four men had come from Winter

Quarters—the last camp of the Saints before the final push through the mountains—with 227 letters, many newspapers and gazettes, bringing the only mail that would get through before the snow made the mountain passes impassable. Another woman wrote of the cost of this mail service. "I paid $1.10 for postage or delivery charges on two letters from friends in the states but did not begrudge it for we were glad to get them."

Even after the mail had arrived in the valley, delivery was by no means prompt or certain. Many of the first arrivals had moved off to distant settlements and were not easily located. In one town the post office was merely a bushel basket in the general store, and anyone who expected or hoped for mail thumbed through the contents until he located his own. In Salt Lake City after the Sunday services in the Bowery, a list of names for whom letters were lying unclaimed, would be called from the platform.

The first letter to leave the valley was written by Father to Ezra Benson about one week after the arrival of the first company. He told of the new settlement in the valley, spoke with appreciation of the fact that every member in the company had come through safely, assured the pioneers on the plains of help, should they need it, and counseled them to be cheerful and praise God for His goodness.

It was much more difficult even to send mail back to the States than to receive it here, since practically all the travel was in this direction. The eastbound mail in the summer of 1849 was carried by Colonel Babbitt, the delegate to Congress from the Territory, and the letters were necessarily sent without benefit of envelopes or stamps, being simply wrapped in buckskin covers and tied with thongs of the same material.

It was almost as difficult to get the mail through to the outlying settlements in the Territory as it was to bring it from the East. One story of the unusual methods of mail delivery, which is only typical of dozens of such cases, is that of the carrier in Kanab. In order to make a short cut and avoid bad roads, a cable line was installed from the bottom of a high precipice to the top, a distance of about one thousand feet. At the top was a windlass to which a long rope was attached with a pulley and hook at the bottom. When the mail was outward bound, the sacks were attached to the hook. A man at the top wound the windlass, and up went the sacks to be replaced by the incoming mail.

Transporting the mails from Missouri to Salt Lake was largely a hit-or-miss proposition until 1850, when a contract was awarded to Samuel H. Woodsen, who in turn sublet it to Little, Hanks, and Decker. A Government contract was no insurance that the mail would come through on schedule, however. There was supposed to be a delivery once a month, but what with riding unbroken Mexican mules over roads that were poor at their best, it is not surprising that the settlers expected the mail carriers when they saw them riding down the hills. It was many years before conditions were bettered to any extent, and as late as the winter of 1858 it required seventy-eight days of hard trail breaking and suffering to carry the mail from Salt Lake City to Independence, Missouri.

Our families had a private post office in Father's offices between the Lion and Beehive Houses. Pigeonholes were arranged alphabetically, one for each member of the family. All of our mail was addressed to "Box B," and mail from Church headquarters bore the same insignia. At one time Richard W. Young was down in Richfield and wrote to me as Miss Klint Chung. At first, no one could locate the lady, but eventually someone figured out that it might be I. Evidently the name appealed to him, for he used it rather a long time in our correspondence.

In the spring of 1860 the age of speed was ushered in by that heroic experiment, the Pony Express. Weeks, actually, were cut from the time formerly required to send a letter when the riders performed the amazing feat of covering the distance from Salt Lake to the frontier in six days.

Stations were built every fifteen to twenty-five miles from St. Joseph, Missouri, to Sacramento, California, where fresh horses and provisions were kept. The rider would leave his station with his precious pouch or saddlebag, gallop like the wind over desert, plain, and mountain ridge, seizing a fresh mount at the station with scarce a glance away from the beckoning trail.

It was no ordinary rider and no ordinary horse that was expected to accomplish this task. The riders had to weigh less than one hundred pounds, consequently they were usually mere lads. They must have unquestioned courage, be excellent riders, and sign Alexander Majors' unique pledge that they would use no profane language, drink no intoxicating liquors, neither quarrel nor fight with other employees, and conduct themselves in every way to win the confidence of their employers. They also received a Bible from Majors which they were pledged to read.

The horses of the quality demanded for the express brought three or four times the price that an ordinary horse sold for. The fact that his pony had been carefully selected and could outrun the Indians' horses, saved the life of many a pony express rider.

The Pony Express was successful beyond the layman's wildest dreams as a means of rapid communication, but as a financial venture for promoters Russell, Majors, and Waddell it was a decided pain in the neck. The expenses ran out of all proportion to the revenue in spite of the fact that the charges for carrying letters were anywhere from one to five dollars for half an ounce. The reasons for this were numerous. It was necessary to keep eighty riders and four hundred horses in

readiness to ride, although there were usually only
about eight men in the saddle at one time. The
riders received from forty to one hundred dollars
a month and were fed and housed at the company's
expense. Hay and grain for the ponies were freight-
ed at a cost of twenty-five cents a pound, outside
of the original cost, which was often very high.
Besides all this, the Indians were constantly burning down the stations and killing or stealing the
ponies. It is estimated that the company lost one
hundred thousand dollars during the one year they
carried on their noble experiment.

By the fall of 1861 the ten-day span of the Pony
Express was made obsolete by the advent of the
telegraph. The first pole for the Overland line was
"planted" on the main street of Salt Lake City,
July 10, 1861, by James Street, general agent for
the company. There was no demonstration at the
time, nor was any particular notice taken of the
event, although the Church and civil authorities
were extremely happy that this great stride was
being made in linking them so much more closely
with the rest of the world.

People in California had been somewhat fearful
that the Indians and the Mormons would jeopard-
ize the safety of the line, but they soon learned
that they had nothing to fear from the latter. Mr.
Street called upon Father, who received him most
cordially and offered him every aid within his
power.

Before long he found that he had need of Father's proffered aid. One of the greatest difficulties the builders encountered was the task of securing poles. There were no trees large enough for the purpose, except in the mountains, and these were not always easily available. A group of the Mormon pioneers had a contract to furnish poles which they refused to fulfill when they found that they were losing money.

Mr. Street apprised Father of the situation and was told in reply that he need not worry; the poles would be delivered as promised. Father then sent word to the contractors that they were to fulfill their agreement if it made paupers of every one of them. Not one man failed to deliver the poles.

The Mormon question was thus very happily disposed of, but a great deal more ingenuity was required in dealing with the Indians, who were at first inclined to greet this new progress of the whites with their usual destructiveness. To meet this situation, Creighton, who was in charge of the east end of the line, had two Indian chiefs send messages to each other over a distance of five hundred miles. Each told the other to meet him at the halfway point, and when the agreement was kept they were certain that the lines were imbued with a supernatural power and consequently worthy of their most wholesome respect.

The lines were completed by October 17, 1861, and the first use was courteously tendered to Father, who sent the following message to J. H. Wade, the president of the Pacific Telegraph Company:

Salt Lake City
Oct. 18th, 1861

Hon. J. H. Wade,
Cleveland, Ohio,

Sir:

Permit me to congratulate you on the completion of the Overland Telegraph Co. line west to this city, to commend the energy displayed by yourself and associates in the rapid and successful prosecution of the work so beneficial, and to express the wish that its use may ever tend to promote the true interests of the dwellers upon both the Atlantic and Pacific slopes of our continent.

Utah has not seceded, but is firm for the constitution and laws of our once happy country and is warmly interested in such useful enterprises as the one so far completed.

BRIGHAM YOUNG

To which President Wade replied:

Cleveland, Ohio,
Oct. 19, 1861

Hon. Brigham Young, President, Great Salt Lake City,

Sir:

I have the honor to acknowledge the receipt of your message of last evening which was in every way gratifying, not only in the announcement of the completion of the Pacific Telegraph to your enterprising and prosperous city, but that yours, the first message to pass over the line, should express so unmistakably the patriotism and Union-loving sentiments of yourself and people.

I join with you in the hope that this enterprise may tend to promote the welfare and happiness of all concerned and that the annihilation of time in our means of communication may also tend to annihilate prejudice, cultivate brotherly love, facilitate commerce, strengthen the bonds of our once, and again to be happy union.

With just consideration for your high position and due respect for you personally,

I remain your obedient servant

J. H. WADE.

Soon after the lines were finished, Father established a private telegraph office in the east room of a little adobe building where the Hotel Utah underground garage is now located, with Willie Dougall as the first operator. Later it was moved to the room just east of the main Church office in the Lion House.

Far more interesting to me than the telegraph office was the room on the west side of the adobe building where Professor Barfoot conducted his wonderful menagerie. The exhibit included such awe-inspiring specimens as a stuffed two-headed sheep and some starfish. In the back yard were beavers, cougars, and other animals from the nearby mountains, safely imprisoned in imposing cages. Ten cents admission was charged to view the menagerie, but one could go in and hear the telegraph tick for nothing.

The telegraph office in Provo was located in the home of Aunt Eliza Burgess, Father's wife, who lived in that city. I spent one winter in her delightful home and remember well the room in the southeast corner of the house which comprised the important "office."

Long before the Overland route was completed, Father had visions of building telegraph lines throughout the Territory. What with colonizing, Indian raids, and the constant influx of emigrants, the need for direct communication was very great. In 1866 the Deseret Telegraph Company was organized, with Father as president, and he immediately sent out a circular to all the Bishops along the proposed route asking them to give the enterprise their earnest support. They responded with their usual enthusiasm, and many people served on the line for months without any pay except in the benefits that came when the work was completed. Father called the men on a "mission" to do this work, much the same as if they were called to go out and preach the gospel.

In October of that same year sixty-five wagons arrived in Salt Lake from the East bringing the necessary wire and insulators, and by December the line was completed between Salt Lake and Ogden. Within another year five hundred miles of telegraph wires had been erected throughout the length and breadth of the Territory and the small, remote settlements brought within direct communication to the rest of the world.

Father also called a number of young people on missions to learn the art of telegraphy and then scattered them throughout the Territory to act as operators. Many of the most efficient of these were young women who carried on their work after marriage with only brief periods off while they had their babies.

One young man by the name of William Bryan

became so adept that Father hired him as his private operator during his trips about the Territory. He was intensely interested in both local and national happenings, and young Bryan would cut in on the wires, wherever they happened to be, and get the news which had been especially compiled for Father by his secretary in Salt Lake.

At one time, when Father and his party had been spending the night at Fillmore, the spring rains had left the roads in an almost impassable state, but as Father was very anxious to get the day's news he said to his operator, "Willie, I wish you would ride on ahead to Scipio and ask Salt Lake for everything of importance as soon as you can without injury to your horse."

Bryan rode to Scipio and found that the nearest approach to the telegraph wires was a good-sized woodpile in the Bishop's back yard. He hunted up the Bishop and told him that he would like some assistance in setting up his apparatus. The Bishop signified his willingness to help, but likewise his doubts of being able to do so successfully.

"Get a table," said Bryan, "and we will put it on top of your woodpile, and I will put my instruments to work up there."

The Bishop brought the table, and in a short time the wire was cut and the instruments installed. Darkness and falling snow soon added to their difficulties, but the Bishop met this situation by bringing a lantern and an umbrella to hold over the diligent operator. By the time Father arrived Bryan was sitting up there in the cold, busily copying the day's happenings as he received them from Salt Lake.

"Say, Willie," called Father, "is that your office tonight?"

"Yes, President Young," he replied, "this is headquarters tonight."

The telegraph brought to an end the necessity of using the Pony Express as a means of rapid communication. However, it could not handle the letters, newspapers, or passengers, and so, for a few years, the stagecoach held the spotlight as the carrier of our still far from daily mail. Russell, Majors, and Waddell lost their mail contract by foreclosure, and it was taken up by Ben Holladay, financier, politician, and sportsman in his own peculiar way.

During the sixties Holladay decided to travel by stagecoach from the Pacific Coast to Atchison, Kansas, a distance of about two thousand miles. He likewise decided to make the trip in less time than it had ever been made before, except by Pony Express, and accomplished his objective by arriving at his destination in exactly twelve days and two hours, beating the regular mail schedule by five days. The trip cost him twenty thousand dollars, and the wear and tear on stock and vehicles, not to mention the wear and tear upon himself. It is the fastest trip on record ever made in a Concord stagecoach.

The Concord coaches must have been terribly

uncomfortable for the long journeys over the mountainous roads. The bodies swung on leather straps, and there were no springs of any description. Nine passengers rode on the inside and one or two on the outside when it was not necessary to carry an armed guard, which was very seldom. The fare from Atchison to Salt Lake was $250, and it mattered not the least whether the passenger weighed three hundred pounds or one third that amount. The lightweight paid just the same as the heavyweight.

As usual, the Indians were the greatest menace the stagecoach encountered. The mail stations were substantial stone buildings with loopholes in the walls for the firing of rifles, and there was always a plentiful supply of rifles. A United States senator once scoffed at the danger of attacks by saying that "the only hostile Indians on the plains were a few kept by Ben Holladay and brought out whenever he needed a new mail appropriation or an excuse for the non-performance of duty." But I rather suspect that the senator didn't take a ride West to prove his contention.

Perhaps, if he had, he would have had the same experience as that of a woman who, a lone passenger in a stagecoach, looked out after an unusually wild ride and found the driver gone. The horses went on of their own accord until the next station was reached, and later the driver's body was found with an arrow through the forehead.

Albert D. Richardson, who came with the Schuyler Colfax party, took a light-minded view of the situation when he wrote of their trip across the plains: "We were a sort of traveling arsenal with two or three weapons to the man. Attacked, we should have been dangerous indeed—if not to the Indians, at least to each other. One night a huge grizzly bear was seated right in our road. His education had been sadly neglected for, with the grossest disrespect to nation and state dignitaries, he refused to budge one inch. So we turned out and gave him a wide berth. Like the man in the story, he was bigger than us and we forgave him."

For a time in 1862, the Indians became so hostile that it was extremely difficult to bring the mail through at all. Stations were burned, coaches robbed, and passengers killed until it became necessary to send out a detachment of thirty armed men from Utah to guard the stagecoaches until U. S. troops could arrive to take the work over. At one place they found twenty-six sacks of mail, a great portion of which had been cut open and scattered over the plains. Letters had been opened and pillaged in such a way as to indicate that renegade whites had been connected with the robberies.

The mail was usually lashed to the bottom of the coaches so as not to discommode the passengers and, after being dragged through numerous mountain streams, frequently arrived in such a sad condition that it had to be hung out to dry before it could be read at all. "We are aware however," said one scribe philosophically, "that it is useless to complain."

After the advent of the railroad, the stage-coaches were still used for many years to serve the outlying towns. Often in this mountain country they carried thousands of dollars' worth of gold dust and bullion. Consequently they were seldom safe from the onslaughts of highwaymen. When they became a rarity, in later years, they brought fancy prices from collectors, the sums paid for them often running into four figures. We had several on our place at one time, but their romantic past meant little to us. We adored them simply because they made such elegant playhouses.

While the trials of getting newspapers printed and distributed compared in no way to the difficulties of bringing the mail across the plains, still they were enough to cause many a headache for the poor printers—for of all the things the pioneers lacked, rags to use in the manufacturing of paper practically headed the list.

During 1846, while the Saints were still encamped in Winter Quarters, with his usual foresight, Father had sent William W. Phelps to Philadelphia to buy a printing press and a full printer's outfit. The press arrived before the first company had left for the mountains in 1847, and with it were a few boxes of type, a meager supply of paper, and some ink. It was no small job to keep the latter from freezing while it was stored in covered wagons or dugouts.

For a full year after the first companies left Winter Quarters, there was no opportunity to send the materials on, and after some thousands of pioneers had arrived in the valley, Father wrote back to Ezra T. Benson, "The people are all wanting you to send on the printing presses, type, paper, ink, etc. that they may begin to receive knowledge once more through the medium of the press and, as you will see, the people are beginning to be scattered into different cities and towns in the valley; and that is the most convenient way of communicating it to them."

It was another two years, however, before the presses could be brought across mountain and plain and put into action. On June 15, 1850, the first copies of the *News* sold on the streets of the city for fifteen cents. Father appointed Willard Richards editor, Horace K. Whitney typesetter, and my cousin Brigham H. Young pressman. Travelers through the city were charged twenty-five cents a copy, but as this sum included the notice of their names, places of residence, and time of arrival and leaving, they probably were fully compensated.

The printers now found that their troubles had only just begun. The pioneers weren't discarding enough rags to keep up the supply of carpets, not to mention having enough left over for the manufacture of paper. What few rags did come in were usually colored, and the printers possessed neither the skill nor the materials for bleaching. The situation became so bad that for a time the paper was forced to come out as a half sheet and that a very dark grey, which caused the editor to lament, "But dark grey is better than no paper, which will soon be the case unless more rags are forthcoming."

I remember so well Brother George Goddard, who used to go from house to house gathering rags for the paper. Mother always dressed me in immaculate white pinafores, and if I happened to tear one she would utter the dire threat, "Brother Goddard will come and pick you up and put you in his rag bag." I took it all very seriously and was frightened to death of him.

In time, paper was shipped in from the States, and the *News* was able to come forth proudly on white paper, also the announcement that "until further notice we are obliged to stop paying cash for rags, but they will be taken on subscriptions to the news and on tithing."

It was all very grand, of course, to have the *News* printed on fine, white paper from the States, but, as usual, the costs of transportation were so excessive that the thirty thousand dollars paid out for paper each year brought only about one fourth of what was needed. The leaders were anxious to begin the printing of schoolbooks and the various Church works. Finally the need became so serious that in 1861 Father imported a paper mill at a cost of between twenty and twenty-five thousand dollars.

This eased the situation considerably, and the

News came out a full sheet, a good color, and with pleasing regularity so long as the water wheel didn't break, the water didn't freeze, or enough rags could be begged or bought at five cents a pound to keep the mill going.

Each change and advance in methods of communication and transportation brought this inland empire into closer touch with the rest of the world until the brightest dreams and hopes of the pioneers were realized by the coming of the railroad in 1869. What it must have meant to my Father can best be imagined, for one of the most tremendous tasks he encountered in the far-flung activities of his career was that of bringing the thousands of emigrants every year over the covered-wagon trails of the West. After twenty-one years of it, he must have been very happy indeed to consign them to the safety and speed of the railroad.

He seems to have had a very definite instinct for railroading, for when he was making his first journey across the plains, he often paused to point out to his associates the route that the coming railroad would use in its course across the continent, and in time the reality proved that his visioning was correct.

Not the least of the advantages offered by the great project was the opportunity given the people of the Territory to work for, and to sell supplies to, the contractors. The situation probably had mutual advantages, for it would have been far more difficult and expensive to import both laborers and foodstuffs than it was to find them right at hand.

Father took a contract for the grading and masonry of 190 miles of road from the head of Echo Canyon to the lake shore. In order to complete the work by the time agreed upon, he needed some thousands of men more than could be spared from the farms, and so he wrote to Franklin D. Richards, in charge of emigration abroad, to make arrangements with the steamship lines so that the emigrants would arrive well ahead of schedule.

"All men physically able to work," he wrote, "will be passed free from Omaha to the terminus and can at the same time travel with their families and friends on the cars, and so on with the trains to this place where they can be distributed on the work required. The number of free passages from Omaha . . . which is in the cash part of the route, will probably enable you to emigrate more than you had anticipated with the money at your command for emigration purposes and will by so much farther aid me in fulfilling my contract."

His contract amounted to about two and one quarter million dollars, and some of this was subcontracted to others, principally John Sharp and my brother Joseph A., who did the heavy stone work of the bridge abutments, cut tunnels in Weber Canyon, and sent men into the mountains to cut timber for ties.

We in Utah watched with avid interest as daily reports came that the shining rails from East and West were drawing closer together. Both sides had their titans of nature to conquer. The Union Pacific had the rugged mountains of Wyoming, through which they must cut a path, and the Central Pacific struggled over the deserts of Nevada where, at times, it was necessary to haul water a distance of eighty miles.

It was at noon on May 11, 1869, when the signal came that the last spike had been driven and the two iron horses stood nose to nose. The national flag was unfurled, the bands played, and salutes of artillery were fired from various parts of the city sending out the glad word that the great work was accomplished. Father was on his annual tour through southern Utah at the time, and therefore was unable to take part in the celebration either at Salt Lake or Promontory.

Father had hoped that the overland railroad would pass directly through Salt Lake City and was very much disappointed when it became definitely known that the route was to be through Ogden, nearly forty miles to the north. However, he was not one to waste time mourning over lost advantages, and long before the completion of the Union Pacific, he made plans to build another railroad connecting the capital city of Utah with the main line.

The Utah Central Railroad Company was organized in March, 1869, with Father as president, and the echoes of the celebration for the overland had scarcely died away before the ground was broken for the new railroad. Father advanced all the money for the preliminary surveys for the first two years, paying the engineers and furnishing all supplies, and none of it was paid back until after all the work was completed. His brother, John W. Young, had direct supervision of the building of the road.

The Union Pacific builders lacked the funds to meet the final settlement with Father and the other local contractors when their work was finished but, as is often the case, misfortune carried a blessing under her dark coat. In lieu of the same amount in cash, they accepted six hundred thousand dollars' worth of rails, locomotives, cars, and other equipment, all of which were utilized in the building of the Utah Central.

The building of the road was another example of the way in which the pioneers co-operated when they wanted to accomplish something really big. Men left their fields willingly to work on the railroad, with pay a most uncertain factor, and the women along the route often left their household duties to go out and prepare feasts for the workmen. Usually the right-of-way was granted without any difficulty, but if it wasn't Father saw that the line went right ahead anyway.

One man, by the name of Wood, had been on a mission, and when he came home and found the railroad running right in front of his house, he simply went up in smoke. He was going to do something drastic to Father—"the idea to usurp authority to build a railroad right past his front porch!" He came storming up to see Father, who, first thing, asked him about his mission. Brother Wood was so angry he wouldn't tell him anything about it. Father said, "All right, we have been hunting for a name for this little place and now we have one. We'll call it Woods Cross." And Woods Cross it is to this day.

The celebration for the completion of the road occurred January 10, 1870. It was frightfully cold, but just the same, people came from all over the Territory to take part in the rejoicing. Father drove the last spike with a steel mallet made of Utah iron bearing on the top an engraved beehive and an inscription—"Holiness to the Lord."

The railroad is said to have been one of the most remarkable ever built in the country in that there were no Government subsidies, no contributions from capitalists, no outside help of any kind. It was built and owned by workingmen.

MANUFACTURING

The Saints were advised by Father before they left Winter Quarters to take with them a few head of sheep as well as the "best tools and machinery for spinning or weaving or dressing cotton, wool, flax or silk or models and descriptions of the same." It was advice which the women of the companies followed to the best of their ability and were glad that they had, for they soon found that clothing fashioned of discarded wagon covers offered little by way either of variety or attractiveness.

For the first couple of years the entire process of making clothing, from the shearing of the wool to the sewing of the garments, took place in the individual homes. When a mother or one of the girls needed a new dress, she took the wool from the backs of the sheep grazing near the house, washed, carded, spun, dyed, and wove it into cloth, and then engaged in the final task of cutting it and sewing it up by hand.

By 1849 one small part of this process was taken out of the home when Amasa Russell built a machine on City Creek for carding wool—said to be the first in the Western part of the country. There was still enough left, however, for the women to do at home that the desire for a new dress was likely to be a suppressed desire as long as necessity would allow.

By this time converts to the Church had begun arriving in considerable numbers from England, and Father had learned that the men from the manufacturing centers had much valuable experience which could be used for the benefit of the pioneers. Consequently he wrote to Orson Pratt in Liverpool saying, "We want a company of woolen manufacturers to come with machinery and take our wool and convert it into the best cloth. We want a company of cotton manufacturers who will convert cotton into cloth and calico and so forth and we will raise the cotton before the machinery can be ready. We want a company of potters—we need them. The clay is ready and the dishes wanted. Send a company of each if possible, next spring. Silk manufacturing and all others will follow in rapid succession. We want some men to start a furnace forthwith, the coal, iron and moulders are ready. We wish the presiding elders of the conference to search out such mechanics as named and have them emigrate immediately."

In another year or so the millers announced that they were able to arrange for the cleaning and combing of the fleeces but warned the women who wished to have the wool carded that they must furnish the necessary grease—one pound to eight pounds of wool and perfectly free from salt. No other part of the manufacture of clothing left the home for some years. Operating the old hand loom was a laborious task, and the equipment in our home was in almost constant use. One year it merited the following announcement in the *News:*

"We understand that Governor Young has a loom in his sitting room in which has been wove by his family more than 500 yards of cloth the present season. If there are any poor folk among us, they need not be ashamed to work. If they are, go and live awhile with the Governor and they will get cured of their laziness. We also understand that the Governor's lady has offered the use of her loom to neighbors who have none, to weave their cloth and board them while weaving."

After the weaving of the cloth came the comparatively simple task of dyeing it. Simple, that is, after various roots and barks had been experimented with to discover what colors they would produce. In order to make the dye, the bark was boiled vigorously until it was rather well softened so that it could be easily stirred and mashed. The liquid would then be run through a sieve, after which it was treated with alum and blue vitriol so that it would harden and "set." Red dye was made from madder root raised in our own gardens, yellow was made from rabbit brush, and the blue came from Dixie indigo. These colors were combined to produce other shades, such as brown and green, although another very pretty shade of green was made from the sagebrush. Black was produced from the root of logwood.

During the late fifties and early sixties a number of woolen mills began operations in various parts of the Territory so that the old hand loom in the front parlor gradually fell into disuse. The spinning wheel continued in very active use, however, for a long time, and homeknit stockings were the rule throughout most of my childhood.

One of Father's greatest hobbies was "home manufacture for home consumption," even when it was not an absolute necessity. His own words on the subject were, "Let home industry produce every article of home consumption." He foresaw at an early date that the breeding of fine livestock would become an important industry in the Territory, and he urged everyone to acquire at least a few head of sheep or cattle. At one time he imported five thousand graded Merino ewes for his own flocks.

In order to provide feed during the winter months, when the wide open ranges were no longer available for grazing, Father experimented with the raising of alfalfa. The seed was planted down at Forest Farm, and when the first crop was ready for cutting, he advertised for someone who knew how to cure the hay. There seemed to be no one who possessed the desired knowledge, so he turned the task over to his overseer, Hamilton G. Park. Brother Park cut the lucerne and straightway stored it away in our capacious barn. He soon discovered, however, that his method was lacking somewhere in the essentials, for the lucerne began to smolder and smoke until, in fear that the barn itself was about to burn down, he dragged the crop all out in the open again.

Even after the weaving of cloth was transferred from home to factory the securing of a new dress was not simple, for it now cost in the coin of the realm what it had formerly cost in time. Perhaps this was one reason for the adoption of the Deseret Costume, which reduced the quantity of cloth required for a dress from upwards of ten yards to between five and seven and also dispensed with girting. Brother Heber C. Kimball wrote, regarding it, to his son, "It makes a wonderful stir with the ladies and is a great relief in expense to the brethren." As a matter of fact, the stir it made with the ladies lasted very briefly for the Deseret Costume was the height of ugliness.

Even in our underclothing we had to economize on cloth, and our pantalettes of unbleached muslin were made with a piece of cambric buttoned on just above the knees—a bit of elegance for the part that might show, only.

For many years every item of clothing that we wore, with the possible exception of an occasional hat—was made at home. Dresses, wraps, shoes, and stockings, all were manufactured on the home lots. It caused us no concern, however, for all of our young friends wore clothing of the same make. Our mothers were wonderfully adept at handling sewing needles or knitting needles, as the case might be.

The furore that was caused when professional bootblacks descended upon the city still causes me amusement, when I think back on it. The idea of paying someone to blacken and shine your shoes! Worse yet, the idea of paying someone the princely sum of twenty-five cents to acquire such trifling additional respectability. "Let the Boot Black Brigade reconsider the situation," protested the *News*, "and lower its prices so that all the people may enjoy its refining offices." Eventually prices were lowered, but it was a long time before anywhere near "all" the people felt constrained to have their shoes polished by other than their own efforts.

Unlike the wool industry, which has remained a basic one in the building of the state, the manufacture of silk never progressed very far beyond the experimental stage, even though the experiment itself was fairly successful. No one knew, for a surety, in those first years just what would grow in the valley and what would not, and Father was anxious to try anything that might aid in establishing a commonwealth.

He sent to France for the first mulberry seed, and when the precious package arrived it contained two or three pounds of what looked very much like mustard seed. It was first planted at Forest Farm, and he had the gardeners prepare the ground with the greatest of care, plowing and harrowing the acre about five or six times. He personally supervised the planting and had them put the seed in so thick that, as one gardener said, "the young trees came up like the hair on a dog's back."

Later on, several more acres were planted, and in 1865 a large cocoonery was built on the farm, and one of the wives, Aunt Zina D., put in charge of operations. The silkworms were also imported from France, and Aunt Zina learned to care for them very successfully. Later on, she went from one town to another teaching the women how to feed and care for the silkworms as well as to try and promote the industry. She had the honor of wearing the first silk dress to be woven in the Territory—woven, believe it or not, on a carpet loom.

After the trees had a good start at the farm, a number of them were transplanted up to our own garden, where Father took great interest in their care. He gave cuttings freely to anyone who would take them, and hundreds of families moved out of their respective front bedrooms and allowed the silkworms to move in.

A small cocoonery was built near the Beehive House, just north of the store. The building was of brick, and the downstairs was used for coal and wood, while the silkworms were kept upstairs under the personal supervision of George D. Pyper, then about fifteen years old and the son of Father's business manager. Later this lad was to become manager of the Salt Lake Theatre and general president of the Deseret Sunday School

Union in all the world. But always he remained, as then, an unassuming, lovable friend.

The process of rearing young silkworms successfully was a very delicate one, and one that I preferred to watch from a distance. The eggs were about the size of a pinhead and had to be kept down in the cellar at a temperature of about fifty degrees until the mulberry leaves had come out. Then they were brought out into the warmth to hatch and placed upon the young leaves to feed. I have heard that the Chinese women place the eggs in their bosoms in order to obtain the necessary warmth for hatching but we, fortunately, had other means at our disposal.

After the worms were hatched they would be placed on the hurdles. The hurdles were frames about three feet square covered with white muslin. Small branches with tender young leaves would be put out for the worms to feed on, and when all the leaves had been eaten off, the debris would be removed.

Five of us girls would come to the cocoonery three times a day to lay the branches out, and when they were bare George would take them out. I tended the silkworms until they made me so deathly sick that Father said I didn't have to do it any more, and I gladly turned the task over to a more stout-hearted sister.

There was a small balcony on the cocoonery, and when George wasn't busy with the worms, he would sit out there and look down into the garden.

He never ventured down, however, because the big, bald-headed eagle was likely to be sunning just below, and distance was a prime virtue where the eagle and young boys were concerned.

Alexander Pyper built a small silk factory on the corner of Third Avenue and Canyon Road where an excellent grade of silk was manufactured. Machinery was imported for winding, doubling, dyeing, and skeining the silk, and cocoons poured in from all parts of the territory to help feed the new venture. Silk handkerchiefs, with a picture of the Salt Lake Temple woven into the cloth, were manufactured there for many years and found a ready sale with the tourists.

For many years exhibits of home-manufactured silk were to be seen at every Territorial or state fair, but after the early enthusiasts had passed on, interest flickered and finally died until all that remains now of a once promising industry are a few rare pieces of "Utah" silk and some scattered mulberry trees.

The raising of sugar beets and the manufacture of sugar was destined to be second only to wool as one of the future great industries of the state which Father sponsored in the early days.

Since sugar was practically an unknown quantity with the first pioneers, the women resorted to every method their ingenuity could devise in order to provide some manner of sweetening for the family food. Beets, squash, and carrots from the garden were boiled down until they produced a dark, gummy substance that imparted some sweetness to the food but little else, in the way of flavoring, that could be called desirable.

During my childhood, while sugar was still scarce, Mother had a round cheesebox that held her allotment for an entire year. We were never allowed to waste any, even after it became plentiful, and if ever I left any syrup or molasses on my plate, it was put away for me until the next meal.

An interesting story told in connection with the scarcity of sugar was related to me of the time when Father visited up in Bear Lake. A friend who spent his boyhood days there stated that "there was no pleasure, there was no satisfaction possible greater than the thought that President Brigham Young was going to visit the community." When the news spread that Father was coming the good people of the town put their heads together to plan how best they could provide for his entertainment. It was decided that he should stay at Pugmire's, since Pugmire undoubtedly possessed the finest home in the valley. Someone had heard that he enjoyed a bowl of bread and milk, and so the one Jersey cow in the county was hastily requisitioned and installed temporarily at Pugmire's. Who had the best chinaware was the next point in order, and the chinaware was exhibited at Relief Society so that a proper choice could be made.

They now reluctantly faced the question of whether or not he used sugar, and if so, what they were going to do about it, since there was no sugar in the valley. Here my friend's grandmother spoke up and proudly announced that she could furnish the sugar. When they raised skeptical eyebrows, she led them into her bedroom and, putting a chair upon the kitchen table, she stood on the chair, cut a hole in the factory that covered the ceiling, and brought down a five-pound salt sack—filled with sugar. In answer to the question, "How did you get it?" she replied, "Every time I have bought fifty cents worth of sugar I have taken one tablespoon and put up there, because in my early childhood I was taught reserve."

While vegetables, melon rinds, corn stalks, and fruit were boiled down to make molasses, such sweetening was of little use for fine cooking or drinks, and the people were about half starved for sugar. Anything that seemed to offer a possibility was seized upon and experimented with. At one time the people of Provo discovered a sticky sap on the leaves and twigs of the trees that had a sweet taste, and they turned out by the score to gather it. The sap was washed from the leaves, after which it was boiled down to syrup and finally to a sort of crude sugar. Since it retained a bitter taste from the leaves and twigs, it was not considered much of a success.

An enterprising citizen of the north end of the Territory tried to make sugar from the sap of the box elder tree in a manner similar to that by which he had formerly made maple sugar in the East. He succeeded in making a syrup and a confection of sorts, but it was a far cry from the refined table sugar that the housewives longed for.

For a long time there was nothing to do but appease the sweet tooth as best one could with molasses and sorghum. The white sugar beet was found to offer the best promise since it could be grown so abundantly, and word was sent to all emigrants to bring a good supply of the seed in order that each family might plant a crop and make enough syrup for its own use.

By 1851 there were three factories in the valley for the making of molasses. Uncle Joseph Young, with two other men, put one up on Emigration Street, one and a half blocks east of City Creek bridge, where they urged all who had a surplus of beets, carrots, or parsnips to bring them along, "well cleaned as for family use and we will make all the molasses we can and return the owners of the vegetables one-half of the molasses made."

It was easily seen that, struggle as they would, the pioneers could produce nothing resembling re-fined table sugar, and once more Father turned to the missionaries in the Old World in the hopes that men could be found who knew the process of manufacturing sugar. In the spring general epis-tle of 1851 he and his counselors stated, "It is our wish that the presidency in England, France and other places should search out such practical op-erators in the manufacture of sugar as fully un-derstand their business, and forward them to this place, with all such apparatus as may be needed and cannot be procured here."

John Taylor, who was in charge of the French mission at that time, took the suggestion to heart and organized the Deseret Manufacturing Company with a capital of $60,000. He purchased machinery in Liverpool at the cost of $12,500 and then paid another $5,000 import duties. As usual, with anything destined for the Territory of Deseret, the initial cost was only a beginning. The apparatus was shipped by boat to New Orleans and thence to Fort Leavenworth, where it was loaded onto wagons drawn by two hundred ox teams for the twelve-hundred-mile journey across the plains.

The heavily loaded wagons arrived in Salt Lake City in the fall of 1852 and for some unknown reason continued on south to Provo. There a heartbreaking discovery was made. By some sad inadvertence the all-important bone-cooking, sugar-clarifying retorts had not been made nor even so much as ordered. The promoters were filled with dismay at having spent a fortune and facing the prospect of having to spend another before they could hope even to begin to operate successfully.

Since the Church leaders had encouraged the venture, they came magnanimously to the rescue and purchased the elephant which was only a shade less than white. As Trustee in Trust for the Church, Father immediately posted notices assuming all equitable claims against the company.

The machinery was hauled back to Salt Lake City, and the erection of a factory commenced on the Big Cottonwood River. In the meantime a portion of the machinery was attached to the waterworks of the public machine shop and utilized in making molasses. Father urged the Saints to plant sugar beets generously, feeling almost certain that they would soon be able to make sugar successfully.

The factory commenced operations in February of 1855, and while hundreds of bushels of beets were run through the French machinery, nothing resembling sugar ever came out—the nearest thing to it being a good grade of molasses.

While this first great effort resulted in failure, the pioneers continued to raise beets and to experiment in the manufacture of sugar until their persistence finally won results and the industry took its place among the great ones of the West.

Father made considerable money during his lifetime in the sense that the term is generally used, and for one brief period he made money literally, as well. The first year that the Saints spent in the valley they managed to get along in fairly good fashion by the age-old custom of barter but, by the end of that year, when their numbers had grown to several thousand, some medium of exchange became almost a necessity. There was a considerable amount of gold dust in the valley, of which a goodly portion had come into the possession of the Church through tithing, and Father made an unsuccessful attempt to turn it into gold coins.

He designed the coins, together with John Taylor and John McKay. On one side the words "Holiness to the Lord" were to be printed, with emblems of the priesthood, and on the reverse side, two clasped hands denoting friendship, with the denomination of the coin. They were to be made in two-and-a-half, five-, ten-, and twenty-dollar pieces. The attempt failed at the start when the crucibles were broken in the first trial.

They then decided to issue paper money in receipt for carefully weighed-out quantities of gold dust, and in a meeting held in the Bowery on December 28, 1848, the people voted authority to Father to issue the new currency bills. Two different types were issued very shortly, the first hand written on safety paper signed by Father, H. C. Kimball, and Thomas Bullock, and the other, printed bills known as the Kirtland bank notes.

For the first few weeks of 1849 Father and his assistants did practically nothing else but "make" money. Bullock would write out the bills, after which Father would sign them, and they would be stamped with the seal of the twelve Apostles. The demand for the bills was so great that often they were forced to work far into the night.

After about ten days of writing the bills by hand, a small printing press was devised for the Kirtland bank notes. Several of the Church officials signed the new bills, and Father imprinted them personally in the new press. Day after day the men worked weighing in the gold and printing and passing out the currency. At last the demand was satisfied and the crude little printing press set aside.

Among the Mormons the paper money was accepted at first without question, for as one writer said, "To those who knew the sound of his voice, Brigham Young's signature made the new money legal by common consent." During the summer, however, when the forty-niners were passing through the valley by the hundreds, they demanded money that could be used in California, which in turn made some of the local merchants doubtful about taking the bills. The High Council handled this matter briefly by recommending that "the licensed butchers who had refused to sell meat for the paper currency be required to do so or give up the butchering business." The butchers decided to accept the currency.

In another six months equipment for making gold coins was perfected, and all the old paper money was called in and destroyed. The engraving on the coins was plain and simple, but as one of the chief mechanics said concerning the dies for the five-dollar pieces, which he personally had made, "If I do say it myself, it was as perfect a piece of money as ever came from a mint."

Even this gold coin was not accepted abroad entirely without prejudice. Merchants attempting to buy goods in St. Louis discovered that their twenty-dollar pieces were accepted at only eighteen dollars, and years later at Camp Floyd the Commandant suggested concerning the five-dollar pieces, "As this coin is understood to be worth only (about) four and a half dollars he recommends to the soldiers not to receive it for more than that sum, and, better still, not to take it at all."

Gold is gold, however, no matter whose name is engraved on the face of the coin, and the Mormon mint continued to do a brisk business with the large amount of gold dust on hand and that which was constantly coming in from California. In time these coins were destined to rise to many times their face value in the collector's kit—had the merchants and soldiers but known it.

Many other industries less important than the ones mentioned here received Father's earnest support and encouragement. It was his constant advice to the people that they not indulge in expensive luxuries that would involve them in debt, but rather produce through their own industry every necessary article for home consumption. He would tolerate laziness in no one, and at one time he wrote: "You know, and my wives and children know that it is in my mind that those who do nothing but sit in rocking chairs can live on potatoes and buttermilk, while those who do the labor should have both the substantial food and the luxuries."

It seems strange, at first glance, that Father should not only have given no encouragement to mining, now the foremost industry of the state, but should have actively discouraged the people either from attempting to dig ore in the near-by mountains or from rushing to the gold fields of California. His reasons for doing so, however, were excellent and showed great foresight.

The pioneers were absolutely dependent upon the foodstuffs they raised in order to sustain life, and they would have been in a sorry plight, indeed, had they turned from raising grain to digging ore. At that time too, of course, freighting was so terribly expensive that it is highly improbable mining could have been made to pay. Besides all this, he had even a deeper reason. It was not his wish that the Saints should acquire great wealth, for their religion had been bought at a tremendous price, and he intended that nothing should come among them, if he could prevent it, that would in any way lessen their spirituality. Speaking in a Sunday meeting of the newly discovered gold in California, he said, "I hope that the gold mines will be no nearer than 800 miles. Prosperity and riches blunt the feelings of man."

Several of the members of the Mormon Battalion had been in California at the time of the discovery of gold at Sutter's mill, and upon their return to Utah some of the leaders urged Father to allow the Saints to move on westward and take advantage of the riches to be found there. His reply was, "If we were to go to San Francisco and dig up chunks of gold, or find it in the valley, it would ruin us. The true use of gold is for paving streets, covering houses and making culinary dishes and when the Saints shall have preached the gospel, raised grain and built up cities enough, the Lord will open up a way for a supply of gold to the perfect satisfaction of his people. Until that time, let them not be over anxious, for the treasures of the earth are in the Lord's storehouse and he will open the doors thereof when and where he pleases."

In spite of this advice, several families joined the ranks of the forty-niners and went on to California, and still others wanted to go but heeded his counsel for "all the Saints to remain in the valleys of the mountains, make improvements, build comfortable houses and raise grain."

Not long ago I was talking with Cyrus E. Dallin, the sculptor, who told me an interesting story concerning his father's attempt at mining in the early days.

Although not a member of the Church, he had come West with one of the companies and settled in Springville. He felt quite positive that there were precious metals in these mountains, but since Father had forbidden any mining he came up to Salt Lake to see what could be done about the matter. The two men sat and argued for a long time, each one being just about as good as the other. Finally Father told Mr. Dallin to go home and come back again after he had had time to think it over. After a short time the would-be miner returned, and Father said, "I have had my secretary write out a permit for you to go into the hills and do some mining. This paper is your permit." He handed him a paper which read, "This permits C. E. Dallin to go into the hills and mine, but absolutely forbids any member of the Mormon Church to assist him." Since there was no one except Mormons in the Territory, Mr. Dallin found his permit of no value.

Mining for coal and iron had been engaged in on a small scale since 1852, but there was no effort to open up the mines to any great extent, beyond what was needed for immediate use, nor to search out the gold and silver deposits which many believed were hidden in the mountains. In 1860 the following item appeared in the *News:* "We have recently been presented with a specimen of virgin copper found in Cedar Valley some ten or twelve miles from Camp Floyd, which those well versed in mineralogy, to whom it has been exhibited pronounce equal to the best they have seen. If it exists in that vicinity, as is alleged, in any considerable quantities, it would probably pay well for working, if any felt disposed to engage in such an enterprise, but in these days, gold is the principal thing sought after and a man who would engage in copper mining in an inland country like this, might by some, be considered in a state of insanity." This is amusing, since this vicinity now boasts the greatest open-cut copper mine in the world.

After the coming of the railroad the mines, naturally, opened up very rapidly. The year before the railroad came through, Utah had two mining districts. Three years later there were thirty-two. Within three months after the driving of the last spike, ten tons of silver lead ore were hauled by ox team to Ogden, where it was shipped to San Francisco, and shortly afterward ten tons of copper ore were shipped from Bingham. Whether or not Father ever looked with any great favor upon the development of the mining industry, I do not know, but at any rate two of the main reasons for his opposition had vanished. The railroad had made shipping a comparatively easy and inexpensive matter, and the people were no longer dependent upon what could be raised on the home lot in order to keep body and soul together.

In equal disfavor with the miners were the doctors and lawyers, but for somewhat different reasons. It was believed that, in the first place, the Saints ought to be able to get along peacefully without recourse to lawsuits and, in the second place, such matters should be handled by the Church leaders and not by professional lawyers. For some time there were no written laws among the pioneers, nor were there any jails. When disputes arose that required the functioning of a magistrate, the elders of the Church sat on the bench and meted out such punishments as fines or public floggings. Not infrequently they were called to act in the cases of emigrants to California who were having trouble among themselves over such matters as a division of chattels, or with the Mormons through trespassing on their property.

When laws and courts finally did come into being, they were shunned by all faithful Latter-day Saints, and on one occasion those who did not shun them quite carefully enough were called to order in a rather severe fashion. During the year 1856 the Mormon spectators had been warned frequently that too many of them were hanging around the courthouse. As they continued to ignore the warnings, Father found other means of removing them, which Heber C. Kimball describes as follows:

"One day Brother Brigham sent Thomas Bullock to take their names for the purpose of giving them missions, if they had not anything to do of more importance. So Brother Brigham counseled me to make a selection—for Las Vegas, some thirty, who are ordered to sell their possessions and go with their families as soon as the weather will permit, for the purpose of going down on the Rio Virgin to raise cotton: another company of forty eight to go down to Green River to strengthen that settlement, make farms, build mills and so forth and some thirty-five or forty to go north to the Salmon river and eight to go to the East Indies. These are all good men but they need to learn a lesson."

If the lesson seems to have been too severe, let it be remembered that this empire could not have been built in the heart of a desert by less rugged and forceful methods and also, that in the great task of colonizing the Territory, men were accustomed to be asked at any time to take their families and possessions and move on to establish another home.

The physicians were held in somewhat higher esteem than the lawyers, and two of them at least, Dr. Willard Richards and Dr. Bernhisel, were among the leading members of the community. Just the same, it was only in the direst extremity that a professional was called upon to administer to the ailing, prayer and good old home remedies finding first favor with the staunch pioneer families. I do not remember of a doctor's being called to our home more than once or twice during my entire girlhood.

Famous among these early-day remedies was a tea made from mountain rush, commonly known as "Brigham Tea." Just how Father learned that this plant had medicinal properties is not exactly known, but it is rather likely that he gained the knowledge from the Indians.

The mineral waters of the warm springs were found, at an early date, to have beneficial values, both for bathing and for drinking, and fortunately they were close enough at hand to be easily available for everyone's use.

On the whole, the Latter-day Saints, then as now, were rather a healthy group of people, due as much as anything, no doubt, to following the precepts of our religion, which forbids the use of tobacco, strong drinks, tea, and coffee.

Even so, I am rather afraid that Mark Twain overstated conditions just a trifle, when he wrote concerning his visit in 1859: "Great Salt Lake City was healthy—an extremely healthy city. They declared there was only one physician in the place and he was arrested every week regularly and held to answer under the vagrant act for having 'No visible means of support.'"

EMPIRE BUILDING

On July 24, 1847, the first company of the Mormon pioneers emerged from Emigration Canyon and gazed upon a broad valley. Most of the little band of 147 souls saw only barren stretches where the one growing thing was the grey sagebrush, but Father must have envisioned a city with homes, green gardens, and fertile fields, for he said with an air of complete satisfaction, "This is the place."

Scarcely had they halted their wagons before they had chosen a site for the Temple, made plans for the laying out of the city, and put their plows into the ground. The last-named effort failed completely, however, until the hard, sun-baked ground had been soaked by the waters of the near-by City Creek Canyon stream.

Attention was then directed toward building the fort, which served as a home for most of them during the first two years. During the trek to the valley the pioneers had been divided into companies of ten, fifty, and one hundred, each governed by a captain, and this same organization continued for a time after their arrival. In building the fort, two "tens" would go to the mountains for logs, staying there for one week at a time. Some of the men would handle the axes, and others would do the hauling, while two or three stood guard for

Indians. Father was counted as one of the best when it came to swinging an ax.

The fort was built in the form of a rectangle and stood on the block now known as Pioneer Square, four blocks south and three blocks west of the Temple. The walls were nine feet high and over two feet thick and enclosed twenty-seven log houses. The houses were built only with an eye to furnishing temporary shelter and certainly afforded but the slightest degree of comfort. The bare ground served for floors, the doors were hung with rawhide hinges, and the windows were covered with anything that the meager contents of a pioneer's wagon would yield. The roofs were of brush covered with dirt, and when the heavy snows fell and melted, the water soaked through onto the hapless inhabitants. If one member of the family happened to be sick in bed, others held utensils over him to catch as much of the water as possible. Swarms of mice and bugs on the inside and the howling of wolves on the outside added to their discomfort.

The following year the city lots were portioned out, and the settlers began to build their individual homes. There were several good reasons for this. The fort, even with additions, had become terribly crowded with the arrival of fifteen hundred more people in September of 1847. Their numbers were large enough now to insure a reasonable degree of safety from the Indians and—the roofs of the cabins began to fall in.

City lots were sold, at first, for $1.50 each, but the farming land was obtained by drawing. No unmarried man could have a lot unless he could furnish substantial evidence that he was intending to marry in the near future. The wards of the city, rather than individual lots, were fenced off in these early days.

Many people remonstrated with Father when he insisted that the streets be made so wide, but he felt sure that the time would come when his stand would be justified. At first, these broad thoroughfares were used for farming with just enough space left in the middle for vehicles to pass through. This practice was somewhat inconvenient for the drivers, however, because there were bars at the end of each street opening into a main thoroughfare, which had to be taken down and replaced each time a wagon went through.

The "city" houses were not a vast improvement upon those built in the fort. The first attempt at making adobe brick failed because there was alkali mixed with the clay which would cause the bricks to expand and burst when exposed to rain. The pioneers finally learned how to make good "dobies," however, and before long many substantial homes had been built in the valley of either adobe or logs from the mountains.

The valley of the Great Salt Lake was Mexican territory when the Saints drove their wagons onto its sagebrush-covered wastes, but Father immediately took possession in the the name of the United

States Government, raised the American flag, and named the territory "Deseret." He was elected governor by a provisional territorial government. Three years later, in September, 1850, Millard Fillmore signed the law creating Deseret a Territory of the United States and—three months after that, the Saints learned about it. It seems that the news was published in the New York *Tribune* and a returning missionary brought the paper home with him by way of the Isthmus of Panama and California. Father was named governor, and his commission was signed by Fillmore and Daniel Webster, who was then Secretary of State. His salary was $3,500 a year, $2,000 of which was to be used for looking after the Indians and for contingent expenses of the Territory. Only two other local men were named as officials. The rest came from the East, arriving in the summer of 1851, after having experienced some serious trouble with the Indians on the way.

During his term as governor, Father created what was probably the original W.P.A. project. He had a mud wall built around the city, ostensibly for protection against the Indians, but in reality to make work for the hundreds of immigrants who had arrived and had nothing to do. The wall was to be twelve feet high and six feet thick at the base. At every forty rods bastions were to be built, with tiers of portholes. The building material was the good earth, wet and reinforced with willows, brush, or anything else that grew along the route. Several gates were planned, one with a highly optimistic eye to the future for the railroad when it should come, and others near the warm springs and City Creek Canyon. The estimated cost was $33,809.78, which may look small alongside of present-day Federal projects but was a goodly sum in that day. The wall was designed to be ten miles long, and much of it was completed, probably all except the portion which was to run along the Jordan River. Of course, it disintegrated very rapidly, but while it lasted it made a splendid place for the boys of the city to play and fight their imaginary battles.

I am quite sure that one of the greatest tasks Father encountered during his strenuous lifetime was that of bringing the thousands of immigrants safely to Zion. For twenty-two years, until the Union Pacific steamed down Echo Canyon, it demanded his constant thought and energy.

Before the Saints had ever left Illinois, he asked them to enter into a solemn covenant that they would never cease their efforts until every person who desired to follow them to their hoped-for haven, and was unable to come by his own means, should be given the opportunity. In 1849 a sum of five thousand dollars was raised for the purpose and christened "The Perpetual Emigration Fund."

The money was lent out to members of the Church who wished to come to the valley and repaid by them after their arrival, as soon as their circumstances would permit.

During the entire journey, companies were under well-organized supervision. In the first great exodus each family was required to have a certain amount of food and other supplies before starting out on the long journey across the plains. In the case of converts coming from Europe, they were first taken to Liverpool in charge of Mormon elders and then put on board ship where they were divided into companies, each company having its own supervisor. Sometimes the ships were chartered almost entirely by Mormon immigrants, several hundred of them being aboard. They would hold daily meetings and provide various forms of entertainment to make the time spent on the long voyage more agreeable.

On reaching America, the same system of supervision was employed both during the railroad journey and the longer trip by wagon from the terminus. Upon reaching Salt Lake City, they were met by Church officials and sent to whatever part of the Territory happened to be most in need of settlers.

Some idea of the great number of pioneers who poured into the valley during the first few years may be gained from the census of 1848, the second year of the settling of Deseret. The census of March, 1848, listed the population of the city as 1,671 persons, with 428 houses erected. The records show that "by Sept. 1848 Brigham Young and Heber C. Kimball had conducted into the valley 3120 persons, 1020 wagons, 205 horses, 63 mules, 3287 oxen, 1682 cows, 518 loose cattle, 1045 sheep, 375 pigs, 1509 chickens, 91 cats, 216 dogs, 6 goats, 20 geese, 7 beehives, 19 doves, 1 squirrel and 5 ducks."

Every spring Father sent out wagon trains to Florence, Nebraska, to carry food to the emigrants along the route. The "church wagons," as they were called, traveled in different units, each with its commander, and took supplies to those who might be in need, as far as the Missouri River.

In 1862 the emigrants' foodstuffs were all drafted because of the Civil War, and it was necessary to send flour and other supplies to them before they could even begin their journey across the mountains. When the train of wagons reached the bridge on the Platte River, an unfriendly bridge keeper refused to allow them to pass over, saying that the timbers in the bridge were unsafe. The Mormons offered to swim their cattle over and roll the wagons across by hand, but the keeper still declined to let them by. They next offered to float the wagons as well and carry the flour over by the sack, but nothing could move the obdurate keeper. He was determined that they should not pass. The Mormons had not brought their flour all this way just to turn around and take it back, however. Under cover of the darkness of night, they took their wagons downstream and searched until they found a sandbar that reached from side to side. Eight oxen were hitched to one wagon and driven into the water at a fast run. Eventually the entire load was crossed over with the loss of but the contents of one wagon. The boxes had been caulked so that the flour was not at all damaged by the water.

The next morning as the cavalcade drove back to the road and serenely past the bridge keeper, the latter gaped at them in amazement and exclaimed, "You d—— Mormons can go anywhere."

Most dramatic of all stories concerning the thousands of men, women, and children who suffered the hardships and dangers of the great trek is that of the "Handcart Pioneers," those valiant souls who, lacking other means of reaching Zion, elected to walk and pull their meager possessions along by hand.

Father had considered this means of transportation thoroughly and believed it to be entirely practical, provided the emigrants followed instructions carefully. Outfits of oxen and wagons were expensive, and many Saints who were anxious to join their friends in the valley were unable to do so because of the cost. The oxen traveled very slowly and held the companies back several precious hours each day. All in all, it was decided to give handcart emigration a fair trial and, accordingly, some two thousand persons reached the valley by this means during the year of 1856.

The handcart was made of hickory or oak and was built the width of the usual wagon so that it could follow in the tracks made previously by the wagon trains. There was a lead cart which carried flour, food, clothing, bedding, cooking utensils, and a tent, and a family cart which carried the remaining chattels, babies, or persons too ill to walk.

The companies were outfitted in Iowa, supervised by men sent from Salt Lake, experienced in the difficulties of trekking over the plains of Iowa and Nebraska and the mountains of Wyoming and Utah. The first companies, who left in June, reached the valley after a hard, but successful, journey and were welcomed enthusiastically by the Saints upon their arrival in the early fall of the year. Late in July, however, two other companies left Iowa who, because of this late start, suffered great disaster before they reached their journey's end. Their cattle were run off by the Indians, and their food supply ran perilously low at an early date. Bedding had been discarded along the way to lighten the loads, and when snowstorms overtook them in the mountains of Wyoming, their suffering was intense. Deaths among them were frequent, and the time finally came when they could push on no farther but sank down to await whatever fate might befall them.

Six hundred miles from Iowa City, Elder Franklin Richards and a group of returning elders had met up with the emigrants and, realizing the seriousness of their condition, had hurried on to report their situation to Father. October conference was in session when they arrived, and Father immediately issued a call for volunteers to go to their assistance. He said to the people, "We want twenty teams by tomorrow to go to their relief. It will be necessary to send two experienced men with each wagon. I will furnish three teams loaded with provisions and send good men with them and Brother Heber C. Kimball will do the same. If there are any brethren present who have suitable outfits for such a journey, please make it known at once so we will know what to depend upon."

The meetings were dismissed, and everyone hurried home to gather food, clothing, and bedding to send with the rescue parties. When they reached the first of the camps, they found half-frozen people who had not eaten for forty-eight hours. Even with this succor, nine more deaths occurred that night.

More wagons and provisions followed, and eventually the survivors were brought into the valley, where all homes were thrown open to receive them and they were cared for most tenderly. It is estimated that about one sixth of the original number of 1,550 persons died on the way.

Additional handcart companies came during the next three years, but by making a start early in the season they came through without any greater mishap than attended other pioneer companies, although, at the best, the system was a very hard one.

The Great Mormon Tabernacle and the Temple located on the same block are two of the most famous buildings in the entire country, and the grounds upon which they stand are visited daily by hundreds of tourists. Since my father was the guiding genius in the erection of both structures, I feel that they deserve a place in any narrative of his life.

The first place of worship built upon the block was the Bowery. When the men from the Mormon Battalion returned during October, Father told them that it was too late to start farming but that they might make themselves useful by going into City Creek Canyon and getting posts for the Bowery.

It was built by the simple method of putting poles into the ground at short intervals, making the framework of a roof—also of poles—and covering it over with branches, sagebrush, or whatever else might be available. There was never better than a dirt floor, and anything that was handy might be utilized for seats, although after a short time crude benches were built.

I liked to go to meeting in the Bowery, because it was easy to see what was going on outside, and this might be entertaining if the sermon was dry. I suppose it was unsatisfactory to the authorities for the same reason. While the Bowery served fairly well as a meeting place in the summertime, it was quite impossible to hold meeting there during the winter months, so, after a few years, the "Old Tabernacle" was built on the space where the Assembly Hall now stands. The Bowery was still used, however, for overflow meetings and during the very hot weather for some years.

The "Old Tabernacle" was commenced in 1851 and finished one year later. It was built of adobes and had an arched ceiling which was supported without pillars. The seating capacity was about twenty-five hundred. Father used the co-operative plan of work in making this building, which was so successful in many of his other enterprises. One group of men cut down trees in the canyons, another group worked in the sawmills, while yet other groups were given the tasks of mixing mortar and making adobes.

About one half of the building was below the surface of the ground, possibly to help solve the heating problem. At the door were two huge brass caldrons filled with water, and near by was a dipper, so that the churchgoers might have a refreshing drink upon entering or leaving the building. There were large chandeliers of glass prisms that sparkled in the light of the oil lamps with a fascinating beauty.

I used to go to church with Mother and divide my time between admiring the glass chandeliers and playing with Mother's pearl-handled fan, which was a very lovely affair made of white silk and edged with swansdown. When both the fan and the glass prisms failed to hold my interest longer, I was given peppermints to keep me from fidgeting.

On the stand, at the west side, was a funny little door which seemed to me far too small for a man to walk through. A few minutes before the services began this would quietly open and Father would appear followed by his counselors and the twelve Apostles. They would take their seats, and then the choir would sing, a beautiful choir of fresh, young voices.

Brother Heber C. Kimball, one of the counselors, was quite bald, and as soon as he had taken his place he would pull a bandana handkerchief out of his pocket and put it over his bald head and down over his eyes. The ostensible purpose was to keep the flies away, but I shall always think that it was so he could sleep through the meeting undetected. I know he always appeared to be rather startled when he was called upon to speak.

The building was equipped with a fine pipe organ, which was run by water power. My sister Fanny played the organ, and Charley Moore did the pedaling. Poor Charley—he was so in love with Fanny that he would pedal for hours, if need be, just to be near her. She was very gifted musically and could come home from the theatre and play through the score of an entire opera after having heard it once. Father had given her a beautiful golden harp which, naturally, she loved dearly. One day he came home and said to her, "Fanny, would you be willing to give your harp to a blind musician?"

Fanny looked up at him very much concerned that her treasure should be threatened, but after a moment's hesitation she said, "Why, yes, Father, if you wish it."

"There is a man by the name of Giles," said Father, "who has just come over from England. Over there he made a living by playing the harp but he was unable to bring one with him. If you are willing, I should like to give him yours." Without more ado, the precious harp which had been hauled a thousand miles over plains and mountains by ox team was given to an almost complete stranger.

Father conceived the idea for the great elliptical, dome-shaped Tabernacle in rather an interesting manner. A convert by the name of Henry Grow arrived in the city from Philadelphia. He had been working for the Remington Company, who owned a patent right for slat bridge construction, and as a compliment to him the company gave him the privilege of using it in Utah, which fact he made known to the authorities upon his arrival here. Father sent him to both the Weber and the Jordan Rivers to build bridges over these streams, using this construction.

After the completion of these bridges, Father complimented Brother Grow very highly on the splendid workmanship which he had displayed, and in a conversation between them one day said, "Henry, I am desirous of constructing a building for our people, anticipating the future numbers, and I have been wondering what plan we should use, for I have built many buildings and no two alike, and I am anxious that this should be different to anything else. What do you think about the

Remington construction? Henry, I had an egg
for breakfast this morning, cooked hard, and in
lieu of chopping it through the center, I cut it
through end-wise and set it up on tooth-picks. I
was strongly impressed that we might use this
plan for the building."

Henry Grow replied, "If you will build me
twelve pilasters, six to a side, solidly constructed
with sandstone and permit me to experiment, as
soon as they are completed I can give you the ex-
treme size of the building which I think can be
safely constructed."

Later on, Brother Grow advised Father that the
building could be safely put up 150 feet wide and
250 feet long. Twelve great sandstone buttresses
were built first and the roof erected by arching it
over between the buttresses. As the work progressed the idea seemed entirely feasible, and so
finally a front and a rear end were added and the
building completed otherwise. The dome is built
with a latticework frame which measures nine
feet from the ceiling to the roof. Only wood was
used in its construction, and because of the great
scarcity of nails, the beams and trusses were held
together with wooden pegs and cowhide thongs.

When completed, the vast elliptical dome rested
upon forty-four buttresses. Between them are
twenty doors, which permit the evacuation of the
building in a very few minutes. The seating capacity is slightly under nine thousand people, but
many more have been known to crowd in upon

special occasions. It was completed in 1867, after having been only three years in the building, a remarkably short time considering the building facilities of the day.

As a child I often went to the Tabernacle with Father and sat with him upon the stand. In warm weather I would carry a palm-leaf fan which I would wave very gently in order that he might give full attention to the speaker, and in winter I would carry his grey shawl, which I would tuck about his knees to ward off the rheumatism. Always I brought along a little bucket of cold composition tea that Mother had made—sweetened, but without cream. This he would drink in place of water while preaching from the stand.

Perhaps an even more amazing feat than the building of the Tabernacle was the construction of the great pipe organ, which, at the time it was built, was the largest in the United States and the second or third largest in the world. Father had often remarked, "We can't preach the gospel unless we have good music," and while he was willing to go to the ends of the earth to get it, if necessary, he eventually found the wherewithal in his own Territory.

A convert by the name of Joseph Ridges came from Australia in 1856. Father learned of his talent as an organ builder before he sailed and sent instructions for him to bring to Salt Lake a small organ that he had made in Sidney. The organ was brought from the West Coast to Salt Lake sealed in tin cases and carried in twelve wagons drawn by mule teams, only to be found unsuitable for use in the great Tabernacle when it arrived. Neither Father nor Brother Ridges were daunted, however, and they set promptly to work to build a new organ out of the materials at hand.

They decided, however, that these materials must be of the best, and so specimens of wood were brought from all over the Territory. Finally from Parowan, some three hundred miles south of Salt Lake, was selected a fine grain of white pine which was free from knots. Thousands of feet of timber were required for the pipes, some of which were thirty-two feet in length, and the hauling of this wood to Salt Lake was in itself a tremendous task. At times there were twenty wagons on the way, each drawn with three yoke of oxen.

Glue was an important item for the construction of the pipes which was very hard to obtain, but this difficulty was surmounted by boiling strips of cattle hides and buffalo skins in large pots over fires. One hundred men were employed for a year doing this work alone. It is considered that if the organ had been bought in the East, it would have cost about $30,000, including the cost of freighting it to Salt Lake. What an amazing picture in contrasts is presented when one realizes that the organ which was built by such primitive methods as hauling timber by ox team and the making of glue from buffalo skins, can be heard in any home in the land by the mere turn of a dial.

As I mentioned before, the first plans for the building of the Temple were made only a few days after the arrival of the first company of pioneers in the valley July 24, 1847. They found but one tree in the entire valley and no green things of any description growing except on the banks of the mountain streams. The people knew they would have to work with all the energy they possessed in order to build shelter and raise enough food to sustain them through the coming winter, and yet only four days later Father, walking about with some of the brethren, struck the point of his cane into the ground and exclaimed, "Here we will build the Temple of our God." Wilford Woodruff drove a stake into the spot, and that very evening a ten-acre block was marked off which was to be the site of the Temple.

Four years later the Saints met in conference and voted to begin building the Temple. They were still destitute and struggling day in and day out to make a home in the wilderness, but they made plans to erect an edifice which eventually was to cost four million dollars and to take forty years to complete. Do I praise too highly when I call such courage and vision magnificent?

In July of 1857, when the news reached the city that Johnston's Army was approaching, only the fifteen-foot wall that surrounds the block and the foundation for the Temple had been completed. When everyone in the city prepared to leave their homes, it was decided that all the work that had been done on the grounds should be entirely obscured. Excavations were refilled and masonry covered up until no vestige remained of the work of years.

After the army had quietly ensconced itself at Camp Floyd the Saints returned to their homes, and shortly afterward building operations were again commenced.

The foundation was first filled with stone taken from near Fort Douglas. When Father found it was rubble, he ordered it all taken out and granite blocks cut.

It was decided that the walls must be of the finest material obtainable, and as a fine deposit of grey granite had been discovered in the Little Cottonwood Canyon, some twenty-five miles southeast of Salt Lake, preparations were made to haul great blocks of this stone to the temple site by the only power at hand—ox teams and wagons. Some of these granite blocks were so large that it was necessary to have four yoke of oxen to bring in a single stone, and that over a period of three or four days. Finally Father decided to build a canal in order that the blocks might be brought down on boats but, before this project could be finished, the railroad had arrived in Utah, and a side line was built to the quarries. Later the canal was used for irrigating purposes.

Father planned the Temple, and the architect was Truman O. Angell, but neither the Temple nor the other wonderful buildings that he planned

Granite blocks for Salt Lake Temple with the newly built Tabernacle in the background

Cutting stone for Salt Lake Temple, Granite Quarry, Little
Cottonwood Canyon

could have been made realities without the whole-hearted co-operation of the people. They were always ready and willing to sacrifice any part of their time and means that might be required for the good of the cause.

For a long time the people who worked on the Temple were paid in "white orders" or "red orders," which meant that they received their compensation in farm produce or meat at the tithing office. The late John F. Bennett, who in time became prominent in merchandising and banking circles, was employed, when a youngster of thirteen, at the Church blacksmith shop, which was organized for the purpose of making and sharpening all the tools used on the Temple. He was given a small wheelbarrow which contained all the weight he could push, and a string with which to lead two blind boys, the three of them having the responsibility of transferring the tools from the Temple to the shop.

For this work he received two and one-half cents an hour or twenty-five cents a day. He only received it, however, until the blind boys became so proficient that they were able to make the trip alone, when he lost his job. Many another man, who later attained wealth and positions of prominence in the state, could tell similar stories of the humble part played in the erection of this great edifice.

The architecture of the Temple combines both the Gothic and Roman in style. Six granite towers surmount the roof, the highest of them measuring 210 feet. On the east center tower stands a figure representing the embodiment of the Heavenly messenger who appeared to John the Revelator and proclaimed the restoration of the gospel. The statue, which is twelve and one-half feet high, is made of hammered copper and is heavily gilded with pure gold leaf.

The walls of the Temple had reached only a height of twenty-five feet when Father's death occurred in August, 1877. It was the greatest of the many buildings he designed. I wish that he might have lived to see it completed.

At the time of Father's death an editorial printed in the *Deseret News* read: "The leading papers of the United States have each published notices, the Cable has flashed the word to Europe, and all parts of the civilized world have been stirred to their depths by the sad news. The name of Brigham Young is familiar all over the globe. His greatness is universally acknowledged, but his goodness is known only to the few."

But that editorial was published over fifty years ago. By now I believe that my father's goodness, as well as his greatness, is universally acknowledged. The historian Orson F. Whitney says of him: "Brigham Young, so long as he lived was the foremost citizen of Utah—not in an official way, but by virtue of his ability, personal magnetism and commanding influence. His position at the head of the church comprising in its

Salt Lake Temple at Night

membership most of the inhabitants of the territory, gave him much of his influence, but not all. He was by nature a leader of men, with a genius of organization and government. With or without office he would have been influential in any community. His power was unusual, but it was one of the forces of his time, and was undoubtedly necessary to the accomplishment of the great colonizing work that he had undertaken."

During his lifetime he peopled this Western territory with about one hundred thousand souls, founded over two hundred cities, established schools, factories, telegraph lines, railroads, and temples. He was dauntless in his great enterprises, fearless in following his beliefs, diplomatic in his dealings with statesmen or Indians—and with his family generous, affectionate, and understanding always. I honor and revere his memory.

Brigham Young At Home

INDEX